REVOLUTIONIZING
RECRUITMENT

KATHLEEN DUFFY

REVOLUTIONIZING
RECRUITMENT

HOW RECRUITMENT RESEARCH IS
RESHAPING THE INDUSTRY

Advantage.

Published by Advantage, Charleston, South Carolina.
Member of Advantage Media Group.

ADVANTAGE is a registered trademark, and the Advantage colophon is a trademark of Advantage Media Group, Inc.

Printed in the United States of America.

10 9 8 7 6 5 4 3 2 1

ISBN: 978-1-64225-1-524
LCCN: 2020923115

Cover design by Carly Blake.
Layout design by Mary Hamilton.

This publication is designed to provide accurate and authoritative information in regard to the subject matter covered. It is sold with the understanding that the publisher is not engaged in rendering legal, accounting, or other professional services. If legal advice or other expert assistance is required, the services of a competent professional person should be sought.

Advantage Media Group is proud to be a part of the Tree Neutral® program. Tree Neutral offsets the number of trees consumed in the production and printing of this book by taking proactive steps such as planting trees in direct proportion to the number of trees used to print books. To learn more about Tree Neutral, please visit **www.treeneutral.com**.

Advantage Media Group is a publisher of business, self-improvement, and professional development books and online learning. We help entrepreneurs, business leaders, and professionals share their Stories, Passion, and Knowledge to help others Learn & Grow. Do you have a manuscript or book idea that you would like us to consider for publishing? Please visit **advantagefamily.com** or call **1.866.775.1696**.

This book is dedicated to all the people who believed and trusted in me. Paula Wright-Tirocchi (who passed away on December 17, 2013) saw something in me that ignited my passion for recruitment. My clients—especially those at the beginning—who were willing to take a risk on a new and different approach to finding talent, many of whom have stayed with Duffy Group since. Duffy Group's past employees—for the role you played in the company's evolution. Duffy Group's current employees—for your unconditional support to the company but most of all to me.

My grandmother, who immigrated to the United States at sixteen from Ireland, and my mom both inspired me to do whatever it took to take care of the family and to be successful. My children, Daniel and Teresa, you are a gift, and I didn't want to miss a moment watching you grow up. My husband, Frank, you moved your art studio from the extra bedroom into the sweltering garage, giving me the space to build Duffy Group. You have been my number one cheerleader.

CONTENTS

FOREWORD

Kathleen Duffy offers an insightful and creative approach to one of the most important business functions that every employer needs: a talented and dedicated employee who is a solid match for the hiring organization. From her early collegiate days, Kathleen had an intuitive sense of what worked—how to conduct research and the essential detailed follow-through. She reflects on how the different leadership roles she had as an undergraduate student always included a selection process for the next cohort of leaders, and so she collectively gained more expertise at each juncture.

As she entered the workforce, Kathleen had the opportunity to learn from the ground up who might be good candidates and to develop key insights from multiple perspectives to match successfully the job candidate, the company doing the recruiting, the work environment, and the culture. Even then she honed her natural talents for helping others recruit the best employees they could. There were many highs and a few lows—the latter being the impetus to pivot in a new direction in her own career by starting a search firm with an entirely different concept.

Recruitment research was developed by Kathleen and further enhanced by her team and colleagues who have since followed her path, and they have found this concept to be more beneficial and cost effective for their clients. The approach, which involves learning more about the organization and its needs and culture, is equally important to identifying the skill set that might be needed in a new hire. With more traditional methods, several candidates might match a skill set but not be a good match for the organization, thus wasting time and resources with an unsuccessful result.

Kathleen's writing style is comfortable and inviting to readers. There is a sense that she is having a conversation with you, providing professional advice while offering insights into aspects of hiring that one would not have considered initially. She strengthens the position by including other professionals who comment on the approach and the various steps involved. Illustrations of actual application also enhance the content of the book. The encouragement that readers can easily move to this type of approach is compelling, and the chapters include questions for one to consider at each stage of the process.

This is an irresistible book that is easy to digest while helping readers to improve their recruitment skills. Having known Kathleen since her collegiate days, I can confirm wholeheartedly that she practices what she preaches. She recruits both through her work and through her numerous philanthropic endeavors and is always strengthening the workforce, whether it be new hires in the workplace or new volunteer leaders to serve on boards.

—Christine Kajikawa Wilkinson, PhD

Senior Vice President and Secretary of the University, Arizona State University

President and CEO, ASU Alumni Association

INTRODUCTION

I connect people.

I connect employers with the skilled, talented candidates who make their organizations even better. I connect bright, innovative professionals with the opportunities that will change their lives.

Making these connections is my passion. It's in my DNA, this ability to connect people in a way that will make organizations stronger and lives better.

When I first launched my recruiting business in 1991 from a tiny home office, employers identified prospective employees using the same strategies they had relied on for forty years or more: placing ads in newspapers, promoting from within, word of mouth, and referrals from current employees. When employers hired outside recruiters or recruitment agencies to identify job candidates, those employers paid a standard, percentage-based recruitment fee, traditionally determined by the candidate's salary or compensation package.

At the beginning, my home office was just a kitchen table and a combination phone/fax machine. But I didn't need high-tech equipment or an ergonomic work space to see that the traditional approaches to recruiting were becoming outdated. I understood that compensation was only one of the factors that determined the right match between employer and candidate, so it should not be the only factor in determining the value of a process designed to identify the best candidate. I wanted a relationship with my clients that was innovative and collaborative; I knew that this had to be reflected in my approach to recruiting.

I didn't set out to be part of a recruitment revolution. I simply wanted to be a good steward of my clients' money.

> **I didn't set out to be part of a recruitment revolution. I simply wanted to be a good steward of my clients' money.**

This is how recruitment research for corporate clients began—from a desire to develop a competitive advantage and from an understanding that not every client is the same and not every candidate search requires the same process. I wanted to offer my clients flexible pricing for my services and a framework that equipped them to purchase only those pieces of the search process they actually needed.

It seems so logical—pay only for the services that you need—but it has revolutionized recruitment. Clients are billed in a manner that enables them to save money, focusing their dollars on the activity that is of most value.

But recruitment research is much more than a new approach to billable hours. It is a collaborative practice that will equip you to make better decisions about how to identify and hire the right people. It is a strategic process that will enable you to both respond to your immediate hiring needs and develop a talent pool to fill future vacancies. And it is a customizable methodology that will guide you as you build data about your business and the people you need to recruit.

I've spent three decades leading Duffy Group, one of the most respected recruiting firms in the country, using my ability to make connections to help individuals find their path and ensure that companies are identifying the right candidates with the best skills.

My mission—and the mission of my company—is to successfully and precisely target the people who are the very best match for my clients' open positions. But it's more than simply finding great employees.

I make a commitment to my clients—a commitment based on trust and focused on collaboration. My clients are entrusting me with one of their most valuable assets—their human resources—and are asking me to partner with them in identifying and acquiring prospective talent. My goal is to honor that commitment through a process that delivers highly qualified candidates who can immediately begin adding value to their new employer.

Recruitment research is both an art and a science. It is a strategic and collaborative approach to uncovering hidden talent using a flexible, multistep methodology. The result? An innovative strategy for recruiting that is efficient, effective, and economical.

I've used recruitment research to help my clients maximize their recruitment resources. This methodology has consistently delivered exceptional candidates while saving my clients up to 50 percent over traditional recruiting fees.

And now I want to share the secrets of recruitment research with you. I want to help you reenvision your approach to hiring, using innovative concepts that I rely on today to recruit for national and international clients in many different industries. These concepts are scalable and economical, helping to identify candidates who are qualified—and interested.

This approach involves five key steps: strategy development, name generation, position promotion, candidate evaluation, and presentation and reporting. Strategy development is where your recruitment process should begin, with a detailed assessment of your current and future needs through specific, targeted questions that provide an understanding of the role, your company, and its culture. Through name generation, you will learn how to uncover *passive* talent (the great candidates who may not be actively searching for a new opportunity) and begin to develop a plan to identify the best people for your organization. Position promotion equips you to gather competitive intelligence and also—critically—to generate enthusiasm for this opportunity. Candidate evaluation shares key insights that will help you develop accurate, detailed assessments throughout the interview process. The final stage—presentation and reporting—is much more than simply concluding your recruitment search with a list of names. In this key stage, you prepare the kind of detailed competitive intelligence that will inform future searches, along with specific assessments of all candidates researched to equip you to meet future needs quickly and efficiently.

In the chapters that follow, I will guide you through each of these steps in more detail, sharing key insights that my team and I have uncovered as we use this methodology to identify the very best talent for an organization or industry. I'll discuss how C-level executives and human resources leaders have benefited from the recruitment research methodology and provide action steps that will equip you to immediately put these principles to work in your organization.

I'll offer insights from other leading recruitment specialists, many of whom share my passion for the recruitment research approach and have discovered its benefits for them and their clients. Recruitment research is a collaborative approach; I'm pleased to bring that same spirit of innovation and collaboration to this book, drawing on the experience and wisdom of other recruitment leaders who have contributed to the recruitment research story.

From a tiny home office in 1991, Duffy Group is now a business that has found thousands of employees for a global network of clients. I launched my company with a focus on recruiting for the financial sector; today, that expertise has expanded to include a team of dedicated recruitment specialists in the fields of alternative and renewable energy, construction, healthcare, manufacturing, higher education, and nonprofit organizations, along with functional expertise in lean six sigma and finance and accounting. Recruitment research is an approach that works, meeting recruitment needs quickly and cost effectively—and it will work for you.

CHAPTER ONE

THE GIFT OF TIME

I was a recruiter long before I even knew it was a profession, long before I recognized the clear value of my ability to identify the right people for the right organization or opportunity. It began when I was in college at Arizona State University (ASU). I arrived on campus knowing no one, but I got involved in a variety of student activities and—perhaps most importantly—I joined a sorority. My experience as a Kappa Delta is what really launched my leadership journey.

On college campuses, fraternities and sororities recruit new members during an activity formerly known as *rush*. Students are invited to attend parties and events and to meet members of the fraternity or sorority, a process designed to inform them about the group's values and culture and to help the organization learn more about this prospective member, equipping each to determine whether they would be a good fit.

Once I became a Kappa Delta sister, I was soon involved in rush, meeting with the girls who wanted to learn more about our sorority and identifying those who would be the best fit. The rush process took place, at that time, two weeks before classes started, during which my sorority hosted hundreds of girls at gatherings designed to give us a sense of who they were and to inform them about our values and community. Especially at the beginning, with a large group of nervous freshmen (and a few sophomores) crowded together, we had a strict time limit on how long we could spend talking to each prospective member in order to ensure that we connected with as many girls as possible. It was noisy and chaotic, with the added pressure of keeping track of those girls who seemed like a good fit and remembering a few key details about each person with whom I spoke. When you're meeting that many girls in the course of a day, and chatting with them for less than five minutes, you need to very quickly decide how or if this person is going to connect with the other members. I discovered that I had a talent for instantly being able to sense that connection and identifying those prospective members who should be asked to join Kappa Delta.

It was an instinct that I now know is a recruiter's gut—identifying that fit and that right candidate. In fact, today fraternities and sororities have abandoned use of the term *rush* for this process of identifying and inviting new members and instead call it *recruitment*.

Long before strengths assessments or career placement tests, I was a recruiter. Those skills that I first honed at ASU inform my decision-making today, helping me to determine whether someone is going to fit into my organization and impacting other areas of my personal and professional life. I became part of the Panhellenic organization on campus, representing the larger sorority community and encouraging young women to participate in sorority recruitment, to meet with other women on campus and find the group that reflected their values and that would provide them with supportive peers and mentors while they pursued their academic goals.

I was also invited to become a Devils' Advocate, a select group of campus ambassadors at ASU and the longest continuously running student group at the university (ASU's mascot is the Sun Devil). Devils' Advocates play a key role in recruiting students to the university, leading campus tours, and providing an opportunity for prospective students and their family members to interact with an ASU student. As a Devils' Advocate, I traveled to high schools throughout Arizona, encouraging the students I met to attend college and—specifically—urging them to become a Sun Devil at ASU.

When I look back at my college experience and all the student activities in which I participated, I can see a clear pattern. I loved connecting the right person to the right opportunity. I was passionate about finding the best people for my organization or community. I was a natural recruiter. But it took me some time to translate that passion into a profession.

I graduated from college in 1981 with a degree in liberal arts. The economy was very challenging in the early 1980s, with few job opportunities, so I accepted a position as the receptionist in the personnel department of a corporation. My typing skills were abysmal, but I excelled at the human resources aspect of working in personnel, especially when it came to hiring. When I met a candidate for an open position in the company, even when someone handed me their application for a job and I had the opportunity to chat with them for a few minutes, I knew. It's the recruiter's gut again—I could quickly identify who would be the right person for many different jobs within that corporation.

I spent about nine months in that job, but there were few opportunities for advancement, and I was increasingly convinced that a corporate setting was not the right fit for me. Several of my friends were working for a boutique recruitment firm—a company that offered a high level of personalized service and that specialized in finding candidates for jobs in specific industries. Through a friend, I was introduced to the woman who was a partner in the firm. Her name was Paula Wright-Tirocchi; she was a well-respected professional, and I immediately knew that she was the mentor I needed to begin my career in professional recruitment. When I learned that there was a job opportunity within her organization, I quickly decided to apply and was ultimately hired as a recruiter.

Fit depends on more than just data, compensation, and expertise. Culture, values, mission, and community are often every bit as important as numbers and work experience.

I spend a lot of time gathering data about organizations and industries to ensure that the firm provides our clients with the very best candidates for each opportunity. But when I look back on this key early step in my own career, I realize how fortunate I was. Fit depends on more than just data, compensation, and expertise. Culture, values, mission, and community are often every bit as important as numbers and work experience. My decision to apply for that first recruiting position was not based on data or career strategy—I admired the partner; I had friends who worked for the company; I liked the office building and location. I was excited to wear a suit to work and to have business cards that identified me as a recruiter, but most of all, I was eager to work for someone who saw my potential and who would make the personal investment in my professional development. These were the factors that shaped my decision to begin a career in recruiting.

It was that partner who identified something in me that suggested that I could be trained to become a good recruiter. Paula taught me the craft of recruiting. She helped me to learn the techniques and provided me with the opportunity to hone them. I still recall our open office setup (referred to as the *bullpen* back in the day); my desk faced hers, and she would monitor my recruitment calls, coaching with phrases like "Say these words …" I discovered that I loved learning about new industries and new technologies. I enjoyed connecting with different people and different companies. Good recruiting involves detective work—identifying the right candidates for a position and then tracking them down—and I loved that as well.

At the time, there were far fewer options available for companies seeking good candidates for open positions. They could place an ad in the newspaper, promote from within, and use word of mouth and referrals. Or they could hire a recruitment firm like ours.

I spent eight years working for that firm, practicing my skills and learning how to be a recruiter. I developed an expertise at making connections within the industries in which our firm specialized. When I needed to find a candidate for an open position, I would talk to my connections, usually by phone, to find out which people at their company might be interested in a new opportunity, learning more about their qualifications and expertise to make sure that they were the right candidates, and then I would contact them to determine whether indeed they were interested in interviewing for a new job. If the answer was yes, I referred them to the appropriate colleague at my firm. There were times when I was working in a new industry and didn't have a network, so I had to build a new one by calling into companies and seeking out the right person to approach about an opportunity—good, old-fashioned cold-calling.

It was a fulfilling time for me, professionally and personally. I got married, my husband and I decided to start a family, and I soon discovered that I was pregnant. Life was very good.

But then I suffered a miscarriage. And the very next month, my employer decided to relocate from Arizona to the Bay Area of California.

By then my roots were firmly planted in Arizona. I loved recruiting, but I did not want to move to California. Fortunately, my firm was willing to hire me on a part-time, contract basis to continue to scout out job candidates by phone, but it quickly became clear that I needed to find some other way to supplement my income. My husband was considering starting his own graphic design and illustration business, so I needed to become the primary earner until his business was up and running. I knew that I was good at recruiting, but we hoped to have more children, and so I wanted the flexibility of being able to work from home.

That's how Duffy Group began. I needed a recruiting firm where I could work remotely while earning a full-time salary. When I couldn't find one, I decided to launch my own.

I knew that it would be challenging to compete with more established recruiting firms, so I began to research different recruiting philosophies and to think strategically about how to develop my own competitive advantage. My original idea was to offer a service similar to the one I offered my former employer: performing the front-end work of investigating and making the initial contact with prospective job candidates before handing off my research to a larger recruitment firm. When I spoke about this service with my dad, who ran his law practice from his home, as well as several consultants who were friends of the search firm and knew my work ethic, I received a lot of positive response, so I knew that there was interest and a potential market for my work.

But I felt that there were additional opportunities—other niches that I could fill. I decided to dive deeper and to learn more about new approaches to recruiting. In doing so, I discovered that not a lot had changed significantly in recruitment since I started eight years earlier. Keep in mind that this was 1991. The internet was not yet mainstream. LinkedIn would not be launched for another twelve years. There was a demand for the kind of research I could provide—the ability to uncover so-called *passive* candidates for jobs—people who were currently employed and not actively looking for a new job but who might be interested if approached with the right opportunity. Most large organizations did not have the time or resources to spend on identifying passive job candidates; their human resources departments were too busy with the demands of managing existing personnel.

The skill of identifying—or *sourcing*—job candidates was quite valuable to these companies. In fact, it was often the most valuable step in the recruitment process. Larger recruitment companies frequently hired smaller companies—or contractors like me—to handle this step for them before they took over to manage the interviewing and hiring process. They then charged their clients a large fee for a fixed package of services; identifying candidates was only one small piece.

I recognized that there was an opportunity here. As I spoke with my connections at various companies, I realized that many were hiring recruiting firms—and paying significant fees—when all they needed was that first step: someone to identify passive candidates who were highly qualified but not actively looking for a new job. Once those candidates were identified, the company's hiring managers could take over, approaching the best candidates on their own, interviewing them, and ultimately hiring the person they selected. They did not need to pay a recruitment firm for these additional steps; what they needed was someone to, for example, identify the top sales managers at their competitors who might be interested in a new opportunity.

Recruitment firms, with their one-size-fits-all model and large fees for a complete package of services, had left an opening that I could fill. I had a specific skill to offer hiring leaders—the same skill I was doing part-time for my former employer. I could assume the front-end recruitment tasks—the initial research—allowing them to focus on the hiring process. In addition, instead of charging a flat fee, I would offer my services on an hourly basis. If clients needed additional support in terms of competitive research or candidate vetting, they could budget for those services, but clients who simply wanted an initial identification of candidates could be confident that they were paying only for the services they needed. It was a model that was designed to save my clients time and money, giving them control over the recruitment process.

I knew that launching my own business was risky. I had never identified myself as an entrepreneur; as a matter of fact, that term was not used the same way it is today. It was reserved for people like Steve Jobs and Bill Gates. But I was an entrepreneur and pioneer, building a business fueled by gut instinct rather than by a well-written strategic plan. I had worked as a professional recruiter for only one small firm. My "office" was a table in my kitchen.

But as I discussed my idea with potential clients, their excitement was infectious. I knew that my plan was sound and that there was a market for the service I was offering.

At the time, I knew only that it made sense to allow clients to pay for just what they needed and that it was easy to pitch the benefits of this customized recruiting to prospective clients. Recruiting managers, small business owners, and corporate HR directors who had often taken on the preliminary work of identifying candidates (at the time, this usually consisted of crafting and placing ads in newspapers, sifting through résumés, making calls to employment agencies, and then verifying candidates) could save time by hiring me to provide those initial research services. Larger firms that were paying significant fees to traditional recruitment agencies could save money by not paying for the steps in the recruiting process that they preferred to manage themselves. They could interview as many candidates as they wanted and retain the list of qualified applicants to use for filling future job vacancies, enabling them to save time and money in making future hires. My clients could better manage the costs involved in recruiting by paying only for the services they needed.

I was excited to get started, confident that I had figured out the ideal recruitment model and the ideal job for myself. Looking back, I celebrate that enthusiasm—but also clearly remember how challenging launching a business was in those days.

Working from home was not as commonplace as it is today. My office technology was a fax machine that operated on the same landline as our home telephone. Sometimes, when the phone rang, I had to yell to my husband, "Don't answer that! It's a fax coming in!" My husband designed business cards and lavender stationery for me—he recommended lavender so that my communications would stand out and be instantly recognizable. If a client was searching for a report or profile of a prospective candidate, it was easy for them to find that lavender document in a crowded file or stack of papers.

I would later discover that others in the recruitment industry were also rethinking the old paradigms of one-size-fits-all packages and exploring more customized services. There were others offering a similar kind of research service—identifying candidates—and working in billable hours, but they were doing what I had been doing before, working as freelancers and selling their research to recruitment firms. But I was no longer a freelancer. I didn't know anyone who was doing exactly what I was doing. I was running my own business, and I was selling my research directly to the companies and organizations that needed it.

My recruiting skills were incredibly valuable as I launched my business, but a key part of successful recruiting is connections—leveraging those you have with individuals and companies and using them to form new connections. My college years at Arizona State University were extremely powerful in this regard, as I had maintained deep ties to the university and to the friends I had made there. One of those friends was a woman I knew from my involvement in Panhellenic activities on campus, Teri Hill—we had been presidents of our respective sororities at the same time. She was working as the head of talent recruiting at American Express. She knew me, trusted me, and was willing to give me a chance. She introduced me to a colleague, Lorraine Field, who listened to my presentation on the services I could offer and the ways in which they could save American Express time and money while getting access to the very best candidates for the jobs they needed to fill. Lorraine liked my proposal and became my first corporate client. She remains a client today.

I recently asked Lorraine what attracted her to my pitch for recruitment research. "Prior to my position with American Express as a recruiter, I was in the search business and was very familiar with the 'research' aspect of the search business," she said. "When I met you and you shared your business proposal to provide research directly to the recruitment team at corporations, I thought it was brilliant. I had many experiences with search firms providing candidates who were not totally vetted or candidates who did not really understand the position for which they were being presented. I usually ended up spending more time with these candidates, recruiting them and determining whether they were a fit, and spending a lot more money with the search firm than I believed they deserved.

"Your model provided candidates who had passed an initial review and then, for a nominal price, were handed over to the recruitment team to manage the rest of the process. I thought (and still think) that this plan was perfect. The hardest part of recruitment is finding the passive candidates. Those are candidates who are not actively looking in the marketplace. As an employer, I want to find those candidates—the ones who might be interested in my company and my opening but are unaware that I have positions available. It's difficult for my recruiters to identify those passive job seekers, and that is where you and Duffy Group offer assistance and partnership. You and your team became an extension of my recruitment team. I really appreciate how you value partnership over profit and often would decline a recruiting assignment if you believed that your services were not cost-effective for the client."

My second corporate client also came from my network. My friend Mark Nelson, who was an executive coach, introduced me to a man who was responsible for directing the executive search strategy for a division of Greyhound that was headquartered in Miami.

Greyhound is known as an intercity bus carrier, but this division specialized in supplying airports with jetways, the ramps that transport passengers between an airplane and an airport terminal building. Their CEO had died suddenly, and the division needed someone to recruit the right CEO candidate from similar organizations.

In those pre-internet days, I depended on my telephone and the library for research. I made a list of other jetway companies and comparable organizations and then called their CEOs. I ended up leaving messages with many administrative assistants. The former CEO had been highly respected in the industry, so in my message I explained that I was recruiting on behalf of Greyhound's division. I noted that they were probably aware that the former CEO had passed away, and I asked if they might be willing to help me in the search for his replacement.

Ninety percent of the CEOs I contacted returned my call. With their help, I was able to assemble a list of qualified, interested candidates in about thirty days (typically, a CEO search using traditional recruiting methods can take months).

My first two corporate clients were thrilled at how quickly and cost effectively they were able to access great candidates. They were my best promoters, telling their friends and colleagues about my services.

This word-of-mouth promotion led to the recruitment leader at Greyhound recommending me to an event management company that was in charge of the halftime show for the Super Bowl. The company needed three or four highly qualified people from other large event organizations to sell advertising, put together events, and bring in more sponsors. It was critical to identify candidates who could quickly begin producing results. Starting with strategy development, I compiled the ten top corporate trade show, meeting, and event planning companies. Next, I called those companies to identify the account managers working with large corporate accounts, such as American Airlines. Once I had a solid list of prospects, I started my outreach, once again using the phone and armed with a great story. Who wouldn't want to work with a company that was producing the Super Bowl? Within thirty days, the client was interviewing candidates and hired three account managers. This was an extraordinary opportunity; my ability to deliver in this new arena cemented my reputation.

In my first year, I went from earning $30,000 to $60,000, and I had a viable business with well-known corporate clients and a proven model for success. By the end of that first year, I had more business than I could handle and knew that I needed to hire additional help.

My first employee was my neighbor, Cathy Wilson. She was working as an executive assistant for a developer who was in the process of downsizing his organization. She began working for me part-time while still working for the developer, quickly mastering the key skills needed for recruiting. It wasn't long before she was working for me full-time. Initially, I trained her in the strategies to perform front-end research, beginning with industry research and identifying our clients' key competitors. Next, I expanded her training to include the more sensitive tasks of contacting candidates and pitching job opportunities to them. She was a natural; very quickly we were both recruiting, enabling the business to service more clients. And just as quickly, we started growing.

I was going to need more help. Many of the people I needed to contact were on the East Coast, so, being based in Phoenix, if I waited to contact them during standard business hours in Arizona, they might be at lunch. To reach them first thing in the morning, I had to start recruiting at five o'clock in the morning. On an average day, I usually worked twelve hours with—if possible—a quick break for a shower. With the business growing, my demanding schedule was, too, and then our son, Daniel, joined our family.

Conveniently, my sister, Sharon, was attending the University of Arizona, so during her summer break, I hired her as a nanny to help with Daniel while I worked. But my son was an excellent sleeper, so while he was napping, I suggested that my sister help me out by answering the phone. Soon I was training her in other aspects of the business, and she gradually transitioned from nanny to recruiter. Today she is one of my star employees.

Duffy Group now employs nearly thirty people. But my sister and Cathy were my first hires, three recruiters working around our kitchen tables.

As the business continued to grow, and my daughter, Teresa, was born, I found myself talking to more women who loved to recruit but who wanted a more flexible schedule. Some were contract recruiters with whom I had worked when I was first starting out in the business. Others were former clients, in-house recruiters and human resources managers for whom I had done research. They knew and respected the work I was doing and understood the benefits of the recruitment model I was using. And they were deeply interested in the opportunity to work from home. Many were mothers who wanted to invest time in both their work and their children. Today, with more employees working remotely and technology facilitating greater connectivity and access to more flexible work spaces, a business whose employees work from home is not the revolutionary concept it was when I first launched my recruiting services. At the time, it simply made sense. In an era before telecommuting was common, they wanted that option, and I knew that, for the right employees, it was an option that would work well.

As a recruiter, I'm sometimes asked how I hire for my own business. It's an interesting question, one that I encourage my clients to think about as they seek to fill vacant positions. What traits must your ideal employee have?

For Duffy Group, it always begins with a shared values system. Because many of my employees work remotely, our working relationship has to be informed by trust and integrity. I look for people who are driven and self-motivated. Some of my hires have experience in recruiting, but they still need to be open to learning—to training in our system and our unique recruitment research model, which I'll discuss more in the chapters that follow. But nearly half of our employees were not professional recruiters when I first hired them. They had honed valuable skills in other industries. One—another neighbor of mine who I first met in an exercise class—was a software engineer; she's now my VP of operations. Another worked as a coordinator in the marketing communications division of a Fortune 500 company. My employees include a former school teacher, a former IT professional, and a former fast-food franchise operator. One of my employees impressed me when I discovered that, as a stay-at-home mom, she had started a dinner theater camp. She would teach the children to cook, help them put together a play, and then they would invite their families to enjoy the food and the performance. I loved her resourcefulness and knew it could translate into excellent problem-solving skills.

That's one of the secrets to great recruiting. You have to be willing to think outside the box, to look beyond traditional sources for job candidates to find someone who will bring the kind of innovation that will help an organization grow. In my case, as I hired people from different industries, they brought in expertise in new areas and helped us form connections and demonstrate expertise that have attracted new clients. And as our team grew, we needed systems to keep our records connected, track clients, and manage billing. We began to hold weekly staff meetings to make sure that everyone was current on our clients' needs and the status of ongoing recruiting projects. Gradually we would also add staff to take care of key administrative tasks like billing, payroll, and collection.

The business I started at my kitchen table has now grown into a thriving recruitment company with a fantastic team. We have found thousands of highly skilled candidates for organizations in many different industries, and the integration of the internet, high-speed modems, and instant access to corporate data has transformed our ability to recruit. I no longer have to drive to the library to research companies. Clients no longer need to look for my lavender stationery; instead, we can email reports and profiles, giving them far faster access to the data they need. We can work more quickly, freeing up time to market our services and promote them to new clients.

Even before the internet revolutionized the industry, our model was simple and effective. Clients who had worked with traditional recruiters were amazed at how much money they could save by customizing the services they hired us to perform and by contracting those services on an hourly basis. Clients who were accustomed to using in-house recruiters and human resources personnel to fill vacant positions were thrilled by the opportunity to access a pool of highly qualified candidates and by the time that freed up for their personnel to focus on other key tasks and responsibilities.

I'm proud of this record. I'm proud of the accomplishments of my team.

But most of all, I'm proud of my role in helping to develop a new approach to recruiting, one that saves my clients time and money, using the skills I first developed on the campus of ASU, talking to girls about becoming a Kappa Delta sister.

Great recruiting is not just about hiring people. The recruitment research model is much more than that. The skills I use every day are skills you can develop to build more effective teams, to identify the strongest leader for today's challenges and tomorrow's opportunities, and to reconfigure groups to better advance a specific mission or achieve a goal. Ultimately, the steps I describe in the chapters that follow are techniques that you can use to more strategically manage your organization's most valuable asset: its people.

Let's get started.

CHAPTER TWO

WHAT IS RECRUITMENT RESEARCH?

There has to be a better way.

Maybe you're a frustrated hiring manager who has filled the same sales position over and over again, only to have employees leave after a year or two. Maybe you're a member of a board that is struggling to find a new CEO to lead a global firm facing significant market challenges. Or maybe you're a human resources leader responsible for quickly staffing twenty key positions for a new facility or clinic.

Traditional recruiting methods have failed to deliver the niche talent or build the talent pipelines you need. You are spending more and more valuable time and ending up sifting through résumés of candidates whose skills and experience aren't the right match for the positions you need to fill. You are paying significant sums for someone else to screen and interview candidates when what you really need is outside-the-box thinking that will identify candidates who can solve your problems.

I understand your frustration. And I have good news: there *is* a better way.

Recruitment research is based on the knowledge that every client has a unique story and unique hiring needs. We launch each search with a focus on identifying those special elements that impact your hiring process. We don't expect you to conform to our recruiting processes; we use a flexible system that delivers exactly—and only—what you require.

Recruitment research is very much a value-added proposition. Our belief is that recruiting should provide flexibility at every stage so that you can determine precisely how we can support your recruiting efforts, whether it's targeting the best people for your organization, promoting an opportunity to qualified individuals, or evaluating candidates through in-depth interviews. Each step of recruitment research is designed to be used either independently to address specific HR and strategic requirements or as part of a holistic approach to workforce planning and recruitment.

As I tell you more about recruitment research, please understand that the purpose of this book is not to criticize traditional recruiting firms or to bash traditional recruitment strategies. I began my recruitment career as a researcher for a traditional recruiting firm—it was actually an executive search firm, specializing in the type of recruiting that targets highly qualified candidates for senior-level and executive jobs. I understand the niche filled by traditional recruiting and respect the recruiters who believe in their approach.

But in the thirty years since I began my recruiting career, I've seen a dramatic evolution in how businesses operate, in how organizations communicate, and in the strategies candidates use to identify new opportunities. Traditional executive search practices have not evolved in the same way. Those practices are still based on a candidate's compensation. As a result, recruiters are significantly motivated in their efforts to help the client find the right candidate from pressure to identify the candidate who will make the most money.

Increasingly, companies are relying on tools like LinkedIn to advertise opportunities to interested candidates. Some organizations are using artificial intelligence (AI) recruitment chatbots, employing AI technology to screen candidate applications, schedule interviews, and answer candidate questions about the position, salary, or work environment.

These approaches have value, of course. With the broad spectrum of hiring needs and recruitment strategies, there's a place for everybody.

But often I hear from new clients that these approaches have not yielded the results they want. They're just not getting the right candidates for the positions they want to fill. They need a partner—someone who will go out and hunt for the best candidates and screen them and qualify them. But they may not need—or want—to pay that partner to interview candidates or to take the final steps to get them over the finish line, because they have the capabilities to do that in-house. Once some of my clients have a short list of interested, qualified candidates, they know how to manage the back end of the process. They can conduct interviews, do background checks, extend offers, and complete the onboarding process. Those clients are eager to purchase and pay for only those parts of our recruiting services that they actually need.

THE TRADITIONAL APPROACH

To help understand what recruitment research is, it may be useful to take a look at what it isn't. Traditional recruiting firms generally use two approaches: *retained search* and *contingent search*. Some search firms offer both types of services while others specialize in one or the other. What's the difference?

Retained search means that the recruiter charges the client a fee in advance to fill a position. This agreement is generally an exclusive one, meaning that the client agrees to fill the position using only that recruiter. The fee is substantial—usually 30 percent, but sometimes as much as 50 percent, of the candidate's first-year total compensation. An initial payment—generally a third of the estimated fee—is required before the search process begins. In exchange, the client receives a short list of qualified candidates (usually between three and ten) to interview. Typically, the second third of the payment is due when this slate of candidates is presented. And the final third of the fee is due when a candidate accepts an offer.

Because this process is expensive, retained search is more commonly used for executive-level positions. Retained search presents candidates who are actively looking for work and also uncovers candidates who are currently employed in comparable roles and likely not looking for another position; that's why this process is sometimes called *headhunting*. The high fees for this search include exclusivity—no other search firm is working on the assignment. Retained search also often includes more extensive research to help uncover other factors that influence a candidate's suitability for a position, investigating details that impact organizational culture and fit. Retained search firms may even create *off-limits agreements*, developing a long-term relationship with a client and agreeing not to recruit candidates from that client for other opportunities.

Retained search firms are frequently specialists in a particular industry or sector. This has advantages—they develop an expertise in the unique needs and requirements of an industry and have at their disposal an extensive network of contacts in that field. But retained search also has disadvantages; for example, a retained search firm specializing in healthcare information technology may not have access to highly trained IT specialists currently employed in the financial sector but who are ready for a new opportunity.

Retained search firms also typically include substantial fees for the research they perform while holding significant control over the candidates uncovered during the search process. Most include a rider in their agreements specifying that, if a candidate presented by the search firm is hired for a different position, a separate fee will be charged equal to 25 percent of the employee's first-year total compensation. Think about that for a minute. You hire a retained search firm to fill a sales director position for your organization. They present you with three or four candidates; you hire one of them and pay the search firm 30 percent of the sales director's first-year salary. Three months later, you need to fill a vacancy for a business development director and realize that one of the candidates you saw a few months ago would be perfect. You now must pay the retained search firm an additional substantial fee, even though no new research is required and the time they need to invest will be minimal.

The contingent search approach is quite different. Contingent firms typically aren't paid until the candidate they provide to a client accepts the client's offer of employment. What does this mean? Put simply: no hired employee, no fee. As a result, contingent recruiters are trying to fill many open positions for many clients at once, using a large database of already identified candidates. Those candidates' résumés are collected based on the stated job requirements and responsibilities and then provided to the client, who will conduct interviews and make a final hiring decision. Contingent search firms generally do not perform extensive research to uncover passive candidates, nor is focus given to factors like workplace culture or fit. The recruiter's mandate is to deliver quick results—providing the client with a list of potential candidates in as little time as possible—since the client is not paying the recruiter for additional time invested in the search and, in fact, may not even pay at all. If you are the client using a contingent search firm, you may simultaneously be advertising the position on LinkedIn and exploring other external and internal hiring options. You can choose not to interview or hire any of the candidates presented during the contingent search.

Contingent firms don't always have the luxury of being able to spend time with the hiring leader or to do any kind of a strategic analysis of the job or the organization. When human resources departments or hiring managers choose to use a contingent firm, they generally select from a group of preapproved contingent firms to use and prepare a job order with the description and requirements, which they submit to anywhere from one to five contingent firms. That contingent firm pulls from its collection of résumés those candidates who meet the advertised job description. It's more of a transactional process than a consultative process.

The contingent firm is more likely to present a large pool of candidates to increase the probability that one will be selected for hiring. Their focus will be on providing you, as their client, with many potential hires rather than only those most qualified for the position. Those firms may be using the same publicly available sources you would—posting opportunities on LinkedIn or other job boards—to target candidates.

When you use a contingent search firm, you are more likely to target people who are actively looking for work. It is an approach often used to quickly fill lower-level positions. Contingent search firms are generally paid 20 to 25 percent of the employee's first-year base salary if their search yields a hired candidate.

I think it's clear that there's a substantial difference between these methods in terms of time spent and fees charged. Those differences have implications, including in terms of trust and transparency, which we'll discuss more in the next chapter. For now, I'll simply say that if you use a contingent search or a retained search firm, you will pay a fee based on a percentage of the candidate's salary. That fee is not based on how many hours the recruiter spends on research, and it isn't reduced if you need only specific stages of the search process performed. It's a one-price-fits-all model.

And that's where recruitment research comes in.

THE RECRUITMENT RESEARCH DIFFERENCE

One of the reasons I've chosen to write this book is because I'm such a passionate advocate for recruitment research. I see the value to retained search and contingent search. I simply think that recruitment research deserves to be globally recognized as a legitimate approach, a third and equally valid path to finding the best people for your organization.

I guess that you could call me an evangelist for this recruitment strategy. It's true—I'm an enthusiastic advocate for an approach that saves my clients time and money. I want you to be able to find the very best candidates—candidates from other industries, candidates from your competitors, candidates who may not be looking for a new job but who will be excited to hear about a specific opportunity that perfectly matches their skills and interests. I also want you to be able to unbundle the search process and to buy only those pieces that you need.

Recruitment research is designed to help you find hidden talent while saving you up to 50 percent of traditional recruiting fees. You can be confident that you are paying only for the effort required and the value delivered. The list of candidates you receive will be carefully curated; only qualified, interested candidates will be presented.

It's important to underscore how valuable those savings are to many of my clients. Duffy Group does a lot of work with nonprofit organizations; those nonprofits are limited in terms of their budget for recruitment. Too often, they have been forced to rely on filling positions through job postings and their own networks. As a result, the candidates they see are mostly active job seekers. Unfortunately, in many cases the right candidates are missing. With recruitment research, they are able to unbundle the process to develop a strategy to target passive candidates that meets their budget and their timetable. Those nonprofit clients are very grateful for the opportunity to partner with a recruitment firm to fill these critical positions—an opportunity that wasn't feasible for them until they learned about the recruitment research model.

I'm fortunate to know many dynamic recruitment experts who share my passion for recruitment research. One is Sheila Greco, president and CEO of SGA Talent.

Sheila's story is similar to mine. She began working for an executive search firm by responding to an ad in a newspaper and gradually, after several years in executive recruitment, shifted her focus to delivering recruitment research to her clients, first as a standalone service and then as part of a broader research and recruitment company she founded.

"I'm always interested in what's coming next," Sheila explained to me. "I'm all about data. I think that data never lies." Sheila notes that this research is really the foundation of everything her firm does, whether it's recruitment, succession planning, or competitive intelligence.

When Sheila and I and a few others began to develop this approach to recruiting about thirty years ago, we were pioneers. But those early novel ideas about unbundling the search process have evolved into a strategic five-step process:

- Step 1: Strategy development

- Step 2: Name generation

- Step 3: Position promotion

- Step 4: Candidate evaluation

- Step 5: Presentation and reporting

Let me guide you through the recruitment research process to explain how it works. In fact, let's imagine that you are a client, a hiring manager eager to partner with Duffy Group to identify the best candidate for your open position.

We will first ask you to complete an in-depth situation assessment. This is much more than a description of the job title, requirements, and necessary skills. We do need to know the responsibilities and requirements, but we also want to understand your organization's culture and personality. We'll ask about the key strategic issues your organization is facing and the factors that might excite a potential candidate about this opportunity. This assessment will provide the basis for the story we will tell about your organization, the narrative that will ensure that your opportunity is presented in the best and most accurate light.

The strategy development phase continues with a conversation—either by phone or in person. We'll ask about your timeline for filling the position and any specific needs you've identified. We'll discuss where you are in the process—have you tried unsuccessfully to fill the position externally or internally? Are there any candidates you'd like us to reach out to immediately? Any industries or competitors we should target?

This phase is a key part of the search process and reflects how recruitment research enables a customized strategy. It's an opportunity for you to identify specifically which steps you want to outsource and which you want to handle in-house. You'll share details about your company and its culture to help us better understand the role and responsibilities of the position for which we're recruiting.

The reason too many organizations fail to successfully fill a job vacancy is because they've reduced the search to just a few words—a job description or a job posting. Those few lines become the paradigm used to assess candidates.

But I prefer a different paradigm, one based on thinking strategically, not only about the basic skills and experience a candidate must have but also about the company culture, the traits of past successful candidates, and the hiring manager's leadership style. By the time this stage is complete, I'll have a detailed picture of what a successful candidate might look like, and I'll also have the key information needed to sell that candidate on the organization and the opportunity.

The second step—name generation—is where the heart of recruitment research takes place. When you hire a recruiter, their mandate is to successfully and precisely target the best candidates for your organization. At Duffy Group, we pride ourselves on our research methodology. We use proven strategies to uncover candidates who are not looking at job boards or posting résumés. And the candidates we uncover for you during the name generation stage become your property. We don't maintain a database of candidates that we circulate again and again to prospective employers. The names we generate for your search provide you with a valuable resource that you can use for other opportunities. You're not just hiring for today; you're also hiring for the future.

You're not just hiring for today; you're also hiring for the future.

The third stage, position promotion, is where we transition from detectives to salespeople. We are representing you, our client, to potential employees, telling your story and getting them excited about the opportunity to join your organization. Candidates who are not looking for a new job need to be pitched, to understand what's innovative and unique about your company and this opportunity. Recruitment research depends not simply on uncovering passive candidates but on telling your story and explaining the important role they can play in that narrative.

In the candidate evaluation stage, we assess candidates using in-depth interview questions based on the knowledge gained during your initial strategy development. Our focus is on asking critical questions to make sure that each candidate meets your specific needs and your organization's culture. Based on this evaluation process, we further prioritize our list of candidates, including only those who most closely fit your specifications.

Recruitment research concludes with a detailed report. You will have much more than a list of names or a file of résumés. This is a real aha moment for many clients. Recruitment research generates competitive data and intelligence that can be used for future recruitment efforts. This research can reveal insights about your competitors' activities and the salaries they are paying employees. It can also equip you with information about strategies and staffing in other industries that may help spark new ways of thinking about your own growth and innovation.

This kind of knowledge delivers a real competitive advantage. And it provides answers to the kinds of questions hiring managers often need to answer. Why aren't more diverse candidates applying for an opportunity? Why aren't there more candidates from public universities? Do we need to offer a relocation package? Recruitment research delivers the data to give a detailed picture of the industry, the talent pool, and the salary and benefit expectations of highly qualified individuals.

HOW IT WORKS

We'll explore each step of the recruitment research methodology in greater detail in the chapters that follow. I'm eager to share these strategies and techniques with you. I'm confident that you'll find value in the recruitment research approach—and I hope you'll also be inspired to think differently about your approach to talent acquisition. I want you to have the tools you need to better support your human resources group, to make sure that you are offering a competitive salary and developing a narrative designed to attract the best candidates. I want to equip you to prepare for future talent needs, not simply to respond to each open vacancy.

Let me close this chapter by sharing a success story, one client's experience that underscores the value of recruitment research. A university was struggling to find a new executive director of development. Fundraising was clearly a critical component of the university's viability, and the right candidate would play a key strategic role. But the position had experienced higher than normal turnover. Attracting a skilled director was proving challenging in a competitive environment. The university had used traditional job postings to advertise the position, but the talent pool was small and qualified candidates seemed reluctant to move to the campus. The university's location—about an hour from the closest major city and nestled among mountains, with extensive recreational opportunities—offered many unique benefits, but housing was much more expensive than in many other college towns.

We reached out to several higher education fundraising professionals and discovered that relocation was going to be an obstacle. But the recruitment research methodology is most successful at uncovering "hidden" candidates and thinking creatively about each opportunity.

Rather than focusing on the job title, we focused on the skill set. We needed to identify candidates who already understood all the benefits of the location, and we realized that this clearly included people who were already living and working there. We wanted candidates who possessed the specific skills necessary to fundraise for a university, and we recognized that local candidates working in the nonprofit sector would demonstrate similar skills at development and fundraising. These highly skilled candidates were not actively seeking a new opportunity, and if they were, they probably wouldn't have looked at higher education job sites to find it. But as we identified key candidates and shared the exciting opportunity at the university, describing the generous benefits, paid holidays, and other advantages of being part of their community, we developed a pool of extremely qualified individuals who would never have been reached through traditional sources, enabling the university to fill the vacancy with a director with established relationships with local fundraising sources and strategies.

A success story? Yes, it is. But it's more. It's proof of why recruitment research works. And recruitment research can be part of your success story, too.

ACTION PLAN

- Analyze your most recent recruiting campaigns. How long does it typically take you to fill vacant positions? How much does it cost?

- Consider whether you need to pay for an off-limits agreement, in which the search firm you hire agrees not to recruit candidates from your organization for other opportunities.

- Determine whether your priority is to have a large pool of potential candidates or a more curated list of only a few highly qualified and interested candidates.

CHAPTER THREE

TRUST AND INTEGRITY

believe in the power of relationships.

In the recruiting world, you'll hear plenty of discussions about the value of leveraging connections, optimizing your network, and weaving professional contacts into your narrative.

Those terms are a little cold to me, and they seem to overlook the critical fact that the resource we're discussing is people.

I want to have a relationship with my clients, one that I hope will extend beyond a single recruiting assignment. And in order for it to be a healthy relationship, and a successful relationship, it has to be based on mutual respect and honest communication.

Relationship experts talk about the importance of a fifty-fifty balance between each partner. But I prefer the idea of a 100/100 equation, where both partners have equal accountability and a shared commitment to making the relationship a success.

That's why I focus so much on recruitment research as a collaborative approach. When my clients are actively involved in our recruitment efforts, when they can see precisely how much time their search is taking through our billable hours, they understand the time and effort we are dedicating to their hiring challenge.

Trust. Integrity. These are vitally important to the work I'm doing and are cornerstones of the relationships I want to build with my clients.

I'm a big fan of Patrick Lencioni. Lencioni is an author and speaker who has written many books on organizational health. He also is a proponent of something called *naked consulting*.

It's a provocative concept, but there is sincere wisdom behind the funny title. Before you turn the page too quickly, let me explain. When Lencioni uses the word *naked*, he's highlighting the importance of transparency, of being real and open and allowing clients to see behind the curtain to fully understand precisely who you are and what you are doing.

Lencioni says that naked consulting succeeds because clients are more interested in transparency, humility, and candor than in perfection, authority, or even confidence.[1] Clients want competence, knowledge, and experience, of course. But they also want a relationship based on trust.

This means being transparent with clients about what we know and what we don't. It means sharing difficult information about a client's industry or competitors. It means equipping clients to more fully understand the work we are doing so that they can decide for

---

1   Patrick Lencioni, "What Clients Really Want," The Table Group, accessed July 2020, https://www.tablegroup.com/hub/post/what-clients-really-want.

themselves whether each step of our service has value or whether there are pieces they discover that they can manage themselves.

By now, you can see that this kind of transparency—this naked approach—is at the heart of recruitment research. And while I'm not quite ready to call myself a naked recruiter, I can tell you that I want my clients to be informed about each step of recruitment research and for my organization to be as transparent as possible about our billing and our work.

THE BENEFITS OF BILLABLE HOURS

As a recruiter, my goal is to get the right person in front of you. My team is talented, smart, and efficient.

There have been times when we've found the perfect candidate for a client in less than forty hours. If we were billing a client a flat fee based on the candidate's salary, that would have translated into tens of thousands of dollars for forty hours of work. But we don't penalize our clients for our efficiency; our rates are an honest reflection of the time it took us to perform the search. In this case, a fee based on billable hours meant that our client saved nearly 70 percent.

Many professionals charge for their services in billable hours. Still, some hiring managers express concern when they first hear about our fee structure. I don't want to start a relationship with a client who is suspicious that they are going to be overcharged, so I make sure that we are as transparent as possible at the beginning. I'm going to be honest with them—if they are seeking an individual with a very specific set of skills and training, if they have geographic limitations or concerns about hiring from competitors, it's going to take time. But they also know that if the search is straightforward, if there is a large pool of qualified candidates, then they will not be overcharged for a search that required considerably less time and effort on our part.

This is another value of the recruitment research method. To clients who have a limited budget and need to be vigilant about costs, I make it clear that one of the key pieces in the strategy development phase—the very first step of recruitment research—is to determine their budget for this search. We understand that not every client has a six-figure recruiting budget. We don't surprise clients with unexpected bills; we provide our clients with regular updates so that they can see and approve each step we are taking on their behalf. Those regular updates detail exactly what activities we are undertaking, as well as the hours spent, so that our clients can see how we are earning their business.

Our updates are also a useful data point for our clients, helping them to understand which parts of the search process are more time-consuming. If, for example, we're working to identify passive candidates in the pharmaceutical industry, it may take quite some time to circle through a company. There are a lot of gatekeepers; it may take longer than expected simply to get past them and to identify candidates. We may spend three hours simply to uncover one potential candidate—and that's before we've promoted the opportunity, determined their level of interest, and vetted them. In those cases, it's quite helpful for the client to see behind the curtain and to assess how much time the process of generating names can take.

Clients may be quite specific about the company they'd like us to target, especially if it's one of their competitors or a market leader in their industry. In those cases, we can do a test, go in and see exactly what is involved in getting beyond the gatekeepers.

Sometimes we then provide our client with an update and say, "This is what five hours' worth of work looks like." In other cases, we report back to the client that we spent several hours unsuccessfully trying to penetrate the gatekeepers. In those cases where we simply cannot reach the people we need to in the organization, we will tell the client so. We may not charge them for that time, since it failed to yield any candidates. But it's a way for us to keep our clients informed, to ensure that they are integrally involved in the process, and it also provides us with an opportunity to reassess the strategy if needed.

In effect, we're acting as key members of our client's human resources team. They can see how many candidates have been contacted, how many are interested, and how many hours are being spent on the search. We want this to be a partnership; we want our clients to be excited about what we are accomplishing, and we want them to be engaged in the process. And if, at any time, they need to pause our efforts, they can do so while paying only for the hours actually spent.

It does happen sometimes—an internal candidate suddenly expresses interest, or a candidate who the client had initially unsuccessfully approached changes their mind and decides to accept an offer of employment. That's good news—for us and for our client. It means that our goal has been achieved: the client has the right candidate for their opportunity. And our client can proceed with the hire knowing that they have not paid a huge investment for a search that was not completed; they have paid only for the hours actually expended for them.

Sometimes we'll share our list of potential candidates with the client before we start the outreach process. This is particularly important when the client is working in a niche industry where they may know the key players. We don't want to waste our client's money by reaching out to a candidate with whom they already have a relationship, someone they could pick up the phone and call. Maybe it's someone they simply forgot about but who would be a great fit for their organization, or a former employee who left for a different opportunity and now has exactly the skills they need. It also prevents us from reaching out to those individuals they do know who they don't want to hire—that doesn't happen often, but we want to prevent any problems before they occur.

This is another important difference of recruitment research. That collaboration, that interaction with our clients throughout the process, ensures that we are adding value to their search efforts. A contingent search might yield a collection of candidates who are immediately disqualified, but the client must spend time sorting through those résumés to weed out unsatisfactory options before being able to focus on the few candidates who meet their needs.

We want to build lasting relationships with our clients so that they will rely on us again and again to help them grow their organization. It's about inclusion rather than exclusion. We want to include hiring leaders and human resources. We're all working together to accomplish the same goal.

These goals are as unique as the relationships we've developed with clients, and they evolve over time. One of Duffy Group's practice leaders has an example of the kind of relationship building that's possible with recruitment research.

"I have one client I've been working with since 2001," she said. "When we began the relationship, they were a start-up organization of twenty people. They didn't even have an internal human resources department. They really viewed me as their human resources department and their recruiting team, and I helped them grow to about one hundred fifty people."

By developing that level of trust, she was able to support the organization through leadership transitions as well.

"One of the owners was looking at stepping out of the president role and asked me to keep my eyes open in case I happened to run across a stellar candidate who I thought could eventually become their president," she explained. "And one day, I happened to talk to such a person. I called the owner and said, 'I've found your next president.' They hired him as a consultant first, and within a year he was promoted to a VP, and within two years he became COO. Within about four years, he became president."

BUILDING RELATIONSHIPS, BUILDING TRUST

Clients often hire us to help identify a skilled professional to fill a sensitive role in their organization. They need a candidate they can trust with confidential information and critical data.

Professionals working in accounting and finance are a great example of the kinds of positions I'm thinking about here. If you are sharing the key metrics of your profits and losses with personnel, you are entrusting them with some of the most important data your business holds.

Duffy Group's Sharon Grace is a practice leader who specializes in accounting and finance recruiting. She views herself as a strategic business partner to her clients; rather than focusing on the short-term transaction of filling an open position, Sharon focuses on building long-term relationships with candidates and clients.

One of her clients is a small CPA firm with no more than ten employees. With a firm that size, their hiring needs are fairly modest—maybe hiring an auditor or a tax expert every few years.

"My first relationship with them was introducing them to a young tax professional," Sharon said. "It was a commonsense thing, building the trust and the relationship, one tax professional, one auditor at a time." That young tax professional is now close to being promoted to partner. The original client is close to retirement. And we've been able to use recruitment research to support them throughout their evolution.

I love stories like this—stories that show the value of our work and highlight the relationships we've nurtured with clients. It doesn't happen by accident. It happens because clients trust us to work quickly and efficiently. They trust our skills, our knowledge, and our ability to uncover the best candidates. They trust the recruitment research methodology. Sometimes they even trust us with their lives.

Eden Higgins, one of Duffy Group's vice presidents of practice development, was in the middle of a weekly update phone call with a client, someone she had been working with for about two years, when he mentioned that he was having trouble seeing his computer screen because he was sitting with his leg propped up on his desk. It was an unusual position, and she remembered it two weeks later, during another update call, when once again the client mentioned that he couldn't see his computer screen; his leg was so painful that again he had propped it up on his desk.

Eden asked him if this was the same problem he had experienced when they last spoke. The client acknowledged that it was, adding that his leg had been bothering him for a month or so. Concerned, Eden asked him if his leg was warm when he touched it.

"When he said it was," she explained, "I told him that he had to get to the doctor right away to get it checked out. I pushed it, telling him that it sounded like it could be a blood clot. 'You need to get it checked out now,' I said."

The next morning, the client texted Eden. Doctors had found that he had deep vein thrombosis, a potentially life-threatening condition in which blood clots form in the deep vein of the leg. Eden's client had several of them.

"I was cursing you all the way to the hospital at ten o'clock last night," the client told Eden, "but I was saying prayers of thanks for you all the way home. You saved my life."

It was an extraordinary demonstration of the value of relationship building, of understanding your client's needs but also connecting with them as a person and caring about their well-being.

"Based on that experience," Eden noted, "he changed his whole lifestyle—working out more, walking more. I'm not sure if anyone in his company ever knew what happened."

Not every client relationship is as dramatic as that one. But in every instance, we want our clients to trust us to support their growth and their success. Our hope is to earn that trust again and again.

As Eden explained, "I told him, 'I'm so thankful I was able to help you. But don't give us work because of that. Give us work because you think that we do our work well.'"

THE NAKED TRUTH

We have a responsibility to our clients to share the information we uncover, even when we know that it may create challenges. Sometimes, in conversations with candidates, we discover that our client's organization may have a damaged reputation that they will need to repair in order to attract top-tier employees. We may learn that candidates with the skill set our client requires will expect a salary twice the amount that our client intends to offer.

We report what we uncover, because we believe that this data will ultimately help our client to develop a competitive advantage. If we can support their efforts to change their narrative, we can better accomplish the goal of adding value to their human resources team and attracting the best candidates to their organization.

Sometimes honesty moves in the opposite direction, and we have to share hard truths about candidates they like and hiring decisions that may prove challenging. Eden Higgins remembers the difficult moment when she realized that a candidate she had presented to a client should not receive an offer of employment.

Eden had worked closely with the hiring leader of a midsize company to identify a candidate for vice president of project finance. It was a niche position that required a specific skill set, and it had taken time to uncover qualified candidates. After a lengthy search, the first two candidates Eden presented to her client received counteroffers or chose to accept other opportunities and declined the offer from Eden's client. Which ultimately led to candidate number three.

When the third candidate was given the offer letter, he deleted one line from the agreement—a line indicating that he would give 100 percent effort to the job. Eden saw the deletion and sent the letter to the client.

"This is candidate number three in a very tough, niche, weird position," Eden recalled. "I called the hiring manager and told him, 'I know this has been a very difficult search for us, and I know that this is the third offer. And I know it's not my company. But if it were my company, I would never want to work with this guy. I think we should rescind the offer and we'll find somebody else better for you.'"

The hiring manager agreed, and Eden was able to ultimately find a candidate who she and the client were confident could fill the position and who was willing to give a full percentage of effort.

These kinds of actions aren't taken lightly. But we have an obligation to our client, and our focus is on building trust in every interaction.

Too often, I hear hiring managers say that they need to do the recruiting themselves because they don't have the budget for a paid search. They assume that the kind of work we do is designed for a different type of client and that recruitment research makes sense only for large organizations or global companies hiring highly paid executives. Maybe you've made this assumption yourself.

The reason I've spent so much time talking about relationship building is because I believe that our clients have value. Each client has unique hiring needs and a specific story to tell.

Each client has unique hiring needs and a specific story to tell.

And recruitment research, with its flexible billing and ability to scale up or scale back, works for all of them.

It works for any business that needs to avoid the inevitable costs triggered when a key role is left unfilled. It works for any business that depends on specific skilled personnel and that can't afford to waste time on extended search processes. It supports businesses that are growing and sustains businesses that need to stay small and agile.

In the next chapter, I'll start to unpack the recruitment research method. And I'll begin the same way that I do with each of my clients: by encouraging you to think strategically about your current and future recruiting needs.

ACTION PLAN

- Determine your recruitment budget. Identify search tasks that you would like to outsource and those that you can handle internally.

- Consider your recruiting priorities. Are there specific competitors you'd like to target? Is diversity of candidates critical?

- Next, analyze elements that may present a challenge to recruiting top talent. Is there a large pool of qualified candidates in your area, or will relocation be necessary? Are you offering a competitive salary and benefits?

CHAPTER FOUR

DEVISE A STRATEGY

My business depends on great detective work. Finding people requires research and investigation, and finding the kind of highly qualified talent our clients want us to identify requires an exceptional focus on the key first step of recruitment research: strategy development.

Thinking strategically about your search process is perhaps the most critical step in recruitment research. When you develop a strategy to grow your business, you'll likely begin by taking a clear and careful assessment of where your organization is today—its customers, its competitors, the services it provides well and those tasks it struggles to complete. Next, you'll identify your priorities and your goals—where you want the business to be next year or in five or ten years. This might also be the time for you to revisit your mission and to assess how well your business supports those values. Finally, you'll reflect on the steps you need to take to achieve your goals and to grow your business in a direction that makes sense for your customers, the marketplace, and your values.

In recruitment research, we use this approach to strategic thinking as a critical launching point for understanding your talent needs and uncovering the person—or people—who will best support those goals. We want to learn everything about your business—your projects and requirements, your corporate culture and personality.

This method of devising a strategy is probably the most important part of the entire process. In our world, it begins with what we refer to as the *intake call* or *intake meeting*. Like a good detective, we use this initial conversation to gather information—information about the client, the hiring leader, the company, the job, the culture, the compensation … everything we need to know in order to sell the opportunity to the potential candidate. But it also provides the road map that we will use to identify who the ideal candidate is so that we can begin to execute on that strategy to hunt and find that candidate. If this step is not done correctly, or if the hiring leader does not give us the time to really understand and uncover all that information, the project is probably going to fail.

In traditional recruiting, this kind of data gathering begins and ends with the job requirements and salary. Of course, we need to understand the skills and responsibilities necessary for the position you want to fill. But in order to deliver the very best value, we want to know more. We want to deeply understand what it is like to be a part of your organization. We want to assess how the right individual will help you achieve your goals. And we want to recognize what's special and unique about your organization—those little-known factors that reveal why a new candidate will be thrilled to join your team.

We call this the *sizzle*. It's the special factor that distinguishes your company or organization from its competitors. It's the unique factor that helps tell your story. We want to fully understand that sizzle, because the sizzle is going to equip us to tell your story to those passive candidates who you want to hire.

The sizzle reveals what's going on with your organization—its key strategic issues. They may be the competitive advantage your company holds in the marketplace. They may be challenges or problems or issues your company will be facing in the next year to five years. They may be something as straightforward as "We're increasing our manufacturing capacity by 100 percent." A manufacturing operations manager might be very excited by that. It's a way of identifying the key issues for the company, for the department, and for the candidate.

The sizzle piece is my favorite part of the strategy development phase. I'm a storyteller at heart, and I love hearing my clients' stories and understanding what makes their business special. I can't wait to find out why a candidate will want to leave their current employer and work for you instead, and it's almost always much more than the simple fact that you might be willing to pay them a higher salary or offer a bigger bonus.

CREATING AN ACCURATE PICTURE

Before our first conversation with a client, we ask them to complete a detailed client intake form. That form provides our first picture of the company, and the data it offers informs our search going forward.

We ask our clients specific questions about their business, their products and services, their revenue, and their key strategic issues. We ask about their company's culture—the values, mission, and daily interactions that shape it as a workplace. We want to know the characteristics and traits of employees who've succeeded in the organization—what made them a particularly good fit? Some organizations do not want an employee who is a smoker or one with visible tattoos. Some nonprofit organizations, because of their mission or values, are looking for a candidate who identifies with a specific faith or is a practicing member of a particular religious group.

Next, we ask questions designed to help us better understand the hiring manager. We want to learn about their background, the departments they supervise, and the tasks those departments perform. Our goal is to learn what makes this department or group unique within the company and the factors that will excite a candidate about joining that team. Understanding how they—the hiring manager—joined the organization further informs our efforts on their behalf.

Why does this matter? The hiring manager will generally be the person we are dealing with, the person on the phone with us. Our ultimate goal is to make their job easier. We view ourselves as an extension of their team. We ask them, at the very beginning, to identify why a candidate would want to work for their company instead of for a different organization. They tell us the story so that we can then tell the story to the candidates we identify.

Using the recruitment research method helps our clients think strategically about themselves and their organization.

These kinds of questions make clear why recruitment research is so unique. We are gathering this kind of data before our first meeting with our clients. We ask these kinds of questions before we even turn our focus to the specifications of the position for which we'll be recruiting. Using the recruitment research method helps our clients think strategically about themselves and their organization.

Of course, we do need to learn about the specific details of the position for which we're recruiting. Traditional recruiting methods often begin here and focus on factors like the job title and location, amount of travel, and educational and professional experience. These details are important, but we want to know more. We ask why the position is open. We ask about recent incumbents—who was successful, who wasn't, and why. We ask the hiring managers to describe the personal style that will fit best within the group. We want to know if there are any unique situations or reporting relationships involved with this position and whether the candidate will assume additional responsibilities or a new role in the future. And we ask about compensation.

Finally, we ask our clients to carefully consider some questions that will play a key role in our strategy development. What have they done to date on this search? Are there specific companies and industries they want us to target? (I'll discuss more about this part of strategy development in the next chapter.) We ask them to identify the title or position their ideal candidate might currently be holding and the kinds of key terms that might be helpful in our efforts to identify the best fit for their organization.

These are the types of questions that should not lead to cut-and-paste answers from a company's website. We need more data, something beyond a "see website" or "see job description" response from the hiring manager. Too often, when a hiring manager is asked to describe their ideal candidate, they'll fall back on generic terms like "We're looking for someone with an entrepreneurial mindset—a go-getter." We use the strategic questions in our intake form to dive deeper and go beyond broad categories to gather the kind of specific, detailed clues that will help us uncover the best fit for the position.

As we discussed in chapter 2, the difference between recruitment research and traditional recruiting firms is the collaboration between the recruitment research partner and the hiring leader. It's a very interactive process. And we really do view ourselves as an extension of their team.

We even ask the hiring manager to describe the interview process and format they will use to screen future candidates. Will they be the first interviewer for the future candidate? Will others provide an initial interview before the final candidate or candidates interview with the hiring manager? The answers to these questions equip us to better support them. Our goal is always to help them be efficient and to provide an economical use of their time and money.

The best thing a hiring manager can do is to take the time to answer these questions, to be thoughtful as they consider how this position informs and contributes to their company's operational goals.

Our focus on strategy development works. I'm proud that so many of our clients not only use us again and again but also are so satisfied with the recruitment research process that they refer new clients to us. One of our clients, the chief operations officer for a medium-size company in the alternative energy industry, said, "I will refer you to people I work with because you all take the time to understand what we need. And if recruiters don't understand what we need, it doesn't work out."

A COLLABORATIVE CONVERSATION

When we begin the search process, we review the client intake form and ask our client to provide thoughtful answers to each of the questions on the form. Sometimes there are multiple managers involved in the hiring decision, or our client prefers to discuss their goals verbally rather than putting them down on paper. In those cases, we'll schedule a conference call focused on gathering the answers to these critical questions.

The phone conversation may take anywhere from thirty minutes to an hour and a half, depending on how many people are participating and the level of input that's needed. Duffy Group's Eden Higgins explains that the information gathered in this strategy development phase serves two key functions: one half of the questions equips the team to find the right candidate, and the other half provides the key data that will sell the candidate on this new opportunity. She subscribes to the idea that what we do resembles skilled detective work. "We're searching and sourcing and sleuthing to find the right person for this position that they have open," she said.

We use the same form for each position, no matter the job, no matter the industry. Even when a client is hiring us to fill multiple roles within their organization, we ask the same questions for each vacancy that they want to fill.

Now, you may be wondering why we do this. Why, when our goal is to provide the best use of our client's time and money, do we ask them these same questions? Why not focus on job-specific skills or emphasize certain questions more for opportunities in healthcare, education, or manufacturing?

The answer is that we want to gather as much data from that conversation as we can. We want to understand their company, we want to understand their needs, and—perhaps most importantly— we want our client to think strategically about what it is that differentiates their company from other companies.

Similarly, we want to encourage our client to identify key characteristics of their ideal recruit, the traits that equip us to then begin our search process. We want to get beyond the basic and boring,

"Where do you hope this employee will be in five years?" We want to understand what a successful first year will look like for the candidate.

Eden has a creative approach to this. She asks the client to imagine that a candidate has been hired and will start tomorrow and then she says, "A year from tomorrow, you're sitting across your desk and you are going to be giving this person a one hundred percent increase in pay and you're also going to be giving them a red Ferrari because they did such a great job. What are the three things that they did? What did they accomplish for you and the company?" Most clients focus on the red Ferrari first—who wouldn't?—but then they begin to consider what a candidate would need to do to earn that car and the 100 percent pay raise. It's a great way to uncover the hidden objectives—the deep strategic needs that every company has and that the very best candidates will be equipped to address.

THE TAKEAWAY

The in-depth questions that we use at Duffy Group to help our clients think strategically about their recruitment needs from the very beginning have practical applications for your business. If you were my client, these are the kinds of questions I would ask you—the type of strategic thinking that can impact your ability to find and hire the best people for your organization.

Whether you need to hire a new executive, build a skilled team for a start-up, or attract committed professionals with key fundraising or networking skills, your most successful strategy will depend on your ability to identify your unique story. What makes your company different? Why should someone jump at the chance to join your team? Which mission will they be supporting that is specific to your organization? What is your sizzle?

Next, think about your top performers—the people who've joined your organization and excelled. Consider their styles, values, and traits. Do you see any points of commonality, and what does that suggest about future candidates you will recruit?

Finally, reflect on Eden's red Ferrari question. What would your next hire need to do to earn that sports car and a 100 percent raise after their first year on the job? How would solving that problem equip your organization to grow and excel?

I know that you're busy. I know that finding the right people is a challenging process. But this kind of strategic thinking matters.

Take the time. Take the time to do this kind of strategic planning, and invite others to collaborate. Make it a conversation—a conversation about what makes your organization special and what makes your story unique. Really be focused and not distracted. Because this is the most important part of the process, and if you don't slow down long enough to spend thirty or even sixty minutes on this critical thinking that will significantly impact your ability to recruit great people, your efforts will not succeed.

ACTION PLAN

- Describe your sizzle.

- Assess who has excelled in the past in your organization—and why.

- Identify the path to the red Ferrari for your next hire.

CHAPTER FIVE

IDENTIFY THE COMPANIES AND INDUSTRIES

F inding great candidates isn't easy.

I don't mean to be silly or flippant with that statement. I'm just reflecting the reality that we see every day. Our clients hire us to do more than fill a vacancy with an employee. They want *great* candidates—people who will support organizational growth and bring unique skills and innovative thinking to each opportunity.

Great people aren't always actively looking for a new job. They are often deeply engaged in their current job. They may not know that you have an opportunity that's a perfect match for their skills; they may not even work in your industry.

And that's where recruitment research steps in.

When you hire a firm like mine to help you find the best candidates for an opportunity in your organization, your goal is to ensure that qualified, talented individuals are identified. This means going beyond people who are sending out résumés and scanning LinkedIn for job postings. You want to uncover those passive candidates who will be ready and able to immediately begin contributing to your organization.

We use the term *passive* to describe candidates who are employed and not actively looking for a new opportunity. Identifying these candidates, the companies for which they work, and the industries in which they operate are critical components of recruitment research.

Why does this matter? Why expand our search to uncover individuals who are already employed and not necessarily eager to leave their job when there are plenty of job hunters ready to explore new opportunities, whose résumés are prepared and polished?

In fact, it's a matter of percentages. According to one recent LinkedIn study, 70 percent of the global workforce consists of passive talent.[2] This means that if you confine your recruiting efforts to people who are actively looking for work, you will reach only 30 percent of the potential workforce. However, the same study notes that 87 percent of both active and passive candidates are open to new job opportunities. It seems clear—if you do the hard work of identifying and uncovering passive candidates, you'll have a larger talent pool from which to draw, and a significant number of them may be interested in that new opportunity when it's presented to them.

We'll talk more about how to promote opportunities to passive candidates later in this book. For now, let's focus on the step of iden-

---

2   LinkedIn Talent Solutions, "The Ultimate List of Hiring Statistics," accessed September 2020, https://business.linkedin.com/content/dam/business/talent-solutions/global/en_us/c/pdfs/Ultimate-List-of-Hiring-Stats-v02.04.pdf.

tifying the right companies and industries where we'll be able to find those passive candidates.

CLIENT EXPERTISE

I'm lucky. My clients are experts in many different industries. They represent some of the leading companies in accounting and finance, alternative/renewable energy, construction, healthcare, higher education, manufacturing, and lean six sigma techniques, among many other areas. They include both nonprofit and for-profit organizations.

I trust their expertise when it comes to knowing their business and understanding their competitors. That's why I invite them to collaborate in the strategic process of identifying the right companies and industries to start our search. In our initial conversation and as part of the intake form, I ask them to recommend companies to target as we begin our recruiting research—and also companies to avoid. Some clients are comfortable hiring from their competitors while others prefer to avoid this.

We discuss the types of departments where their ideal candidates might be working as well as what their title or position might be. We ask them to share any contacts they may have at those companies they'd like us to target—we always are looking to identify not only potential candidates but also potential channels into an organization who might be able to jump-start our search and speed up our process. Because our goal is to save our clients time and money, we're eager to find ways to move past the gatekeepers to more efficiently reach those qualified candidates.

Finally, we ask our clients to share as much information as possible about their competitors. Do those competitors rely on a few key individuals to drive revenue? What is their reputation in the industry? Is their leadership diverse? Have they hired others from that particular organization, and if so, were those individuals successful in their new position?

These insights equip us to identify likely companies and industries to start our search. But that's only the beginning.

OUR EXPERTISE

These company and industry leads from our clients inform our search, but this initial information is simply the framework we use to guide the early stages of our recruiting efforts. It's worth noting the dichotomy in our search: while we are hunting for *passive* candidates, our search is extremely *active*, and it begins with outside-the-box thinking about where we might identify those candidates. We think about the conferences and associations relevant to our client's industry, considering where professionals in that field might be gathering, sharing innovative ideas, and networking. Those associations are a rich source of data—data that we can use to build our list of target companies and organizations.

Our goal is to understand who the ideal candidate is and then to think creatively and strategically about where that candidate might be found. They may not have an obvious job title or occupy a linear position. But we use key terms to map out our search and then start the hard work of digging.

The work we do is customized, and it's strategic. Sometimes hiring managers present us with a fairly generic job description—for a marketing manager, for example. That generic job description has failed to produce the results they want. They're not seeing the right candidates for their job postings, through employee referrals, whatever the means they're using to push out awareness of that job. That's where our expertise comes in.

The client may know that they want to hire a marketing manager, but our sourcing can help them discover whether they need a candidate skilled at digital marketing, project management, or brand strategy. Our client may be entering a new industry and not know the key players. They are relying on us to find out. Through these conversations, and our regular reports, we can learn more about the kinds of candidates who will best meet their needs—candidates who may be demonstrating their marketing skills in a different arena from the space our client occupies.

Sometimes our clients are very specific about the companies that they want us to target. And sometimes they'll say, "You can look in the local area and find anybody who makes sense out of similar companies." Or they might say, "We're not sure. We've just started looking for somebody with the skill set and we're pretty open about where you can look."

When I describe recruitment research as strategic, this is what I mean. We have to develop a strategy for each search. We need to determine whether our search will be local, regional, national, or international. We need to develop a list of potential target companies. And even if we know what companies to target, we still need to plan strategically to find the right locations, the right contact information, and the right people to approach.

NARROWING THE SEARCH

Each search that we do is unique. For some organizations, there is a lot of synergy with other companies and even industries, so we are able to sift through a wide network. For others, our search has to be much narrower and targeted, because the skills needed for a particular opportunity are very specific.

The latter usually involves those kinds of highly technical positions where you must have a particular knowledge base and critical training to move a process or a project forward. When you have that kind of an individual contributor, where the knowledge is often proprietary and even confidential, your search will be specific to that particular industry. Often there are far fewer candidates to approach, and their expectations for salary and benefits will be much higher in order for them to consider a new opportunity.

When you are hiring for business and support roles, you have a broader pool of candidates to approach, so our focus is on carefully considering our client's goals and objectives. Is your goal to increase your sales by 100 percent? It may make sense to look for a salesperson who is successfully selling a similar product. But what if your goal for this salesperson is to perform at a very high level selling your product to a specific director of procurement? Then we can consider candidates who already sell to that director of procurement, a search that might take us to different industries with the same target market and the same target buyer within that company.

We also think about your mission as we identify companies and industries. This is particularly true when we want to fill CEO and senior leadership roles in the nonprofit space. It can also be true in higher education, but again, it depends on the role and the specific and unique needs of our client.

As you can see, it all comes back to customization. We don't create artificial targets or limit our search with meaningless goals. We don't say, "We have to target this many companies," or "We must expand our pool by adding at least one additional industry." That might lead us away from our goal of saving our clients time and money. We expect to spend at least ten to twenty hours on critical research like this before we ever speak to a potential candidate.

I'm always excited to learn from other recruiting experts who are thinking creatively about the work that we do. Kelly Renz is president and CEO of the recruitment research firm Novo Group. Kelly explained to me, "Research is not just a list of candidates when done right. It's a highly targeted set of profiles that accelerate the selection process significantly and at a fraction of the cost of retained search. Clients don't have to sift through an enormous list of names like the research of the 1990s. Profiles are more highly matched and accurate with today's tools and approaches—it's quality over quantity, which saves time and money." Kelly's firm spends time targeting nontraditional sources for talent searches—looking at online specialized groups, speaking engagement rosters, and professional organization memberships.

Amanda Piriano, president and managing director of Thorn Network, is another expert in recruitment research. I asked her if there was one fact that she wished prospective clients knew about recruitment research. Her response? "That we are not an agency with a database. Each search strategy is created based on the variables of the client and search parameters targeting the employed, passive candidate who is typically not on the market."

You can't take a passive approach to recruiting passive candidates. As Amanda noted, "We are proactive (vs. reactive) in all our business practices focused on solving the problem in front of us. And we value personal communication (in person or verbal, over the phone) versus written communication in all areas of business."

You can't take a passive approach to recruiting passive candidates.

A recent survey profiled in *Harvard Business Review* highlighted the importance of this kind of careful and customized approach to developing a talent pipeline, and the results were not surprising to those of us who believe in the power of recruitment research.[3] The data in this survey showed that companies that successfully recruited, specifically in the digital space—speaking with qualified candidates who have the right skills, experience, and education—were not following the traditional path of targeting candidates who worked for the competition or who graduated from top-tier schools. Instead, they looked for potential, not credentials, and considered candidates holistically, assessing their ability to work as part of a team rather than simply studying their individual qualifications. The companies that experienced success emphasized the importance of ensuring that their search was as broad as possible, uncovering candidates in unexpected schools, companies, and industries. The result? A workforce that is skilled, creative, and also considerably more diverse in terms of gender, ethnicity, and socioeconomic status.

PRACTICE LEADER

I'm fortunate to have a team of experts who know their industries well and who are highly skilled at finding the right candidates. We use the term *practice leader* as a way to highlight this expertise.

In our organization, a practice leader is an individual who is a senior, well-experienced recruiter and who is developing a practice of their own within our infrastructure. This is an opportunity for

---

3   Jeff Kavanaugh and Ravi Kumar, "How to Develop a Talent Pipeline for Your Digital Transformation," *Harvard Business Review*, November 27, 2019, https://hbr.org/2019/11/how-to-develop-a-talent-pipeline-for-your-digital-transformation.

recruiters with entrepreneurial spirit to shape their own business, using our back office to provide support resources.

Our practice leaders have built strong relationships in specific industries. They know where to find the qualified professionals who can best fill opportunities. They've chosen their industries or specialties because these are areas about which they are passionate. They understand the competitive landscape and are able to anticipate what potential candidates might think about an organization. Some of my practice leaders have been recruiting in their industries for twenty years or more, so they've developed clear areas of expertise. This springboards the growth of their practice, because they are recognized as experts and authorities in those respective spaces.

We aren't unique in developing this kind of expertise. Many recruiters focus on specific industries or on specific levels of staffing needs. What *is* unique is our model. Recruitment research equips us to approach each search a little bit differently and to deliver specific and customized market data to our clients.

Let me give you an example. Sometimes we receive an RFP from a potential client, a formal document inviting us to prepare a proposal or bid to provide recruiting services.

When these come in, it's usually a clue that this potential client is accustomed to the traditional retained search model. They're expecting a proposal or bid that requests 30 to 35 percent of the candidate's compensation, paid in thirds, going from start to finish of the search.

Let's imagine that they are looking for a hospital CEO. They will ask us, "How many searches have you done for CEOs of hospitals in the past five years?" We can answer those questions, and we can share how many searches we've performed for hospital CEOs as well as related searches that have filled key positions in healthcare settings.

We can discuss the data that we generate and the value of our search process.

Sometimes these clients are not in a position to think strategically; they've been given a specific procurement goal or have artificial restrictions placed on their recruiting decisions. They might speak to a firm that has performed eighteen hospital CEO searches in the last five years and place greater weight on the number of searches than on the market research that accompanies the search.

I understand those kinds of decisions. It's why I've said that there is space for different approaches to recruiting.

But it's also why I'm proud that such a large percentage of our business—more than 70 percent—comes from referrals and recommendations. Clients who respect our work—and the recruitment research model—share their understanding of its value with others.

Again and again, clients will praise this new approach to recruiting. A new client will mention hearing about our methodology from an existing client. Often they will specifically mention a practice leader who fully understood what they were looking for and who was able to help them completely navigate the market in which they were operating, providing critical data that informed their decisions about salary, benefits, and even the type of candidate who could best meet their needs and the industry in which they might be found.

Our goal is to provide excellent service to our clients, to make them feel comfortable. There's even a bit of chemistry to it. Practice leader Eden Higgins had a conversation with one well-connected client in which they discovered that they shared a passion for "companies that have cool technology and cool people." As they chatted, they discovered multiple points of agreement in terms of precisely who and what qualified as *cool*.

After the conversation and a successful recruiting search, Eden noted, "Now he knows how we recruit. He knows what I recruit in. And he knows that if he thinks people are cool, I probably would, too. So he's going to refer. He knows that we take the time to figure out what the company needs and how it works. And then we find the right people who will fit in."

SURVEYING THE LANDSCAPE

By the time we begin to have conversations with potential candidates, we understand the landscape in which they are operating. We have a clear picture of the industry, the key players, and our client's identity in that space.

As our client's representative, we develop research that not only will help them respond strategically to their current search but also will support their efforts to build a talent pipeline for future vacancies.

Duffy Group Practice Director Melissa Barker is an expert in corporate recruiting research and successfully sourcing targeted competitors for candidates. She stresses the importance of developing the kind of market data integral to the recruitment research model.

Melissa worked with a property management client who was establishing a presence in the Denver area. They had not previously operated in the Colorado market and so didn't know their competitors and didn't have a firm handle on salary expectations in the region. That's where Melissa began, by gathering the kind of competitive intelligence and market data to inform their recruitment efforts.

"Part of what I delivered to them along the way is information I've gathered from people I've talked to," Melissa explained. "They now know who their biggest competitors are, they know what they're paying, they know what the title of the corresponding job in their company is, and that's helped them build out their management structure with new communities as they take them over."

CONSIDER YOUR OWN LANDSCAPE

I said it at the beginning of this chapter: it's not easy to find great candidates. Recruitment research requires strategic thinking, careful planning, and creative problem-solving.

It's not work that just anyone can do. That's why our clients are loyal to Duffy Group and recommend us to others. But there are elements to this kind of strategic thinking that you can use as you think about team building and identifying talent in your organization.

First, *try to avoid typecasting*. Your next COO may have a completely different background from the one who most recently held that title. They may be working for your competitor, or they may be in a different industry. They may be younger or older. They may hold a different degree. They may have earned experience in a smaller company than yours or one much larger. Expand your definition of who can fill key roles in your organization.

Next, *be realistic about your opportunity*. Know your competitors, research the salaries they are paying, and learn as much as you can about your organization's reputation in its industry. If you are entering a new market, make sure that you understand the people as well as the products. Gather the data that will equip you to identify who the best people are in your field and where they are working.

Finally, *look for potential, not credentials*. The best candidate for your organization may not be working for the competition. They may not have a graduate degree from a top-tier school. Focus more on the skills you need in a candidate than on where those skills were first identified.

As you can see, it's about more than thinking strategically. Recruitment research also depends on the ability to think creatively.

ACTION PLAN

- Identify your key competitors and the strategic differences between their workforce and yours.

- Develop a holistic picture of your organization's reputation in its industry.

- Assess and consider how to respond to typecasting tendencies in your senior management roles.

CHAPTER SIX

TALK TO THE RIGHT PEOPLE

I don't waste time.

When I first talk to new clients about the methodology of recruitment research and my use of billable hours, one of their most common concerns involves time management. They understandably want to know where my time will be focused and what oversight they will have to ensure that the dollars they spend are directed toward their specific recruitment needs.

It makes sense that new clients require this reassurance. I'm representing a brand-new way of thinking about recruiting. I understand my clients' desire to have a better sense of control over their hiring process, and so I invite them into a conversation about our progress and the data we're uncovering.

One of the clearest ways I accomplish this is through regular reports, usually weekly, which specify the steps we are taking on their search and the time those steps require. I want my clients to collaborate on this process, as I've mentioned before, and one of the most direct ways I can engage with them in our efforts is through regular status reports that clarify what is unfolding as a result of our recruiting efforts.

Management experts often talk about the difference between informing and communicating. Informing doesn't invite collaboration; telling people a series of facts doesn't engage them. My goal is to share the insights we uncover so that my clients can ask questions and can actively participate in the strategy we've developed.

That's why I believe that communicating our progress through regular updates is so critical. It creates a sense of teamwork and underlines the fact that we are working hard to be an extension of their human resources management team.

But what about those potential clients who question the focus on research, who examine the hours we spend on identifying the right companies and industries before speaking with a single candidate and want to fast-track the process to generate an immediate list of names? Well, recruitment research isn't for everyone. It can be useful to think about your recruiting goals in order to identify the strategy that will produce the results you want. Is your goal to quickly have a long list of names and résumés to review, even if many of those candidates will prove not to be a good fit? Or is your goal to end the search with the very best candidate for your organization, plus valuable data to support future talent needs?

These early hours spent making sure that we are talking to the right people are an investment, but it's an investment that will save you time and, I believe, money. We spend those hours at the beginning of the search to save hours at the back end.

When I first started in recruiting, it was challenging to actually connect with the right people—to get past the gatekeepers who answered phones and screened incoming messages and were charged with directing calls to the appropriate person.

The landscape looks different today. There are fewer secretaries and assistants answering phones, and it's easier to connect directly with the passive candidates we are targeting. People are accustomed to being contacted; they are more comfortable sharing their cell phone numbers and generally answer their own phones. In those cases, our research concentrates on uncovering personal email addresses and cell phone numbers. There are still a few industries where you need to get past gatekeepers—higher education is one example—but for the most part, technology has accelerated our ability to connect directly with potential candidates.

Technology also supports our research efforts. LinkedIn is one platform that has revolutionized our business. But LinkedIn is just a tool; it's not the complete and total answer to recruiting needs. Too many businesses—in fact, too many recruiters—rely solely on LinkedIn, believing it is the only way to recruit. But it's not.

First, it's worth noting that you have to register to be on LinkedIn, and some busy professionals have not taken the time to set up a profile. Sometimes a highly qualified individual has omitted a keyword from their LinkedIn profile, which prevents them from appearing in a search. We've also noticed that the algorithms may impact your ability to connect with certain candidates. LinkedIn is structured based on your connections to other people and whether you're connected to them directly—be it a first-level connection, second-level connection, more remotely, or not at all; if you don't have those common connections, you may not see every candidate. We've experimented with paid recruiter accounts and standard LinkedIn accounts and noticed that sometimes we find candidates with the standard accounts who aren't turning up using the paid recruiter accounts and vice versa.

The bottom line is that we need to do more than simply type a few key words into LinkedIn. If it's a local search, we need to scour local sources. We need to look at the Business Journals Book of Lists, we need to check out the Chamber of Commerce, we need to do Google searches.

If your goal is to uncover highly qualified passive candidates, there are no shortcuts. You need to really dig in and understand the full scope of who is out there.

CONSIDERING COMPANY CULTURE

A key part of talking to the right people is making sure that any candidates we approach will be able to quickly and successfully integrate into our client's organization. That's why several of the questions on the intake form we ask clients to complete focus on organizational culture.

What do I mean by an organization's culture? In essence, your organization's culture is the underlying principles, beliefs, and values that serve as a foundation for your corporate decision-making, whether we're talking about customer service, or new product introductions, or sales techniques, or any of the countless strategic actions that your company undertakes and the policies it enacts.

A focus on company culture is certainly not unique to Duffy Group; it's something of a hot topic in HR circles. Spend a little time on LinkedIn and you're certain to find articles on culture and fit. Most companies are eager to share their mission statement, their values, and the foundation of their corporate culture. But it's a bit more challenging to identify the candidates whose own values and personal goals will align with those of our clients.

The research makes clear why it matters, why it's critical for you to spend time considering culture and fit when you are evaluating new hires for your organization. Employees whose values are most consistent with the culture of their organization have greater commitment to their employer, are less likely to leave after two years, and have higher job satisfaction. Those same employees perform their jobs more successfully, are more likely to collaborate with others to complete tasks, and receive better job performance ratings.[4]

It's worth noting here that there can be a difference between the culture that's acknowledged—the one that's highlighted on websites and promotional materials—and the actual organizational culture. That's why I encourage clients to think carefully about the early questions we ask and to answer as honestly as possible.

For some clients, their corporate culture can be very loose; for others, it's quite specific and narrow. And for a few international clients, their culture varies depending on which location has the opportunity they need to fill.

One of our clients is a manufacturer of high-end kitchen and bathroom appliances, a global organization with thousands of employees. Duffy Group partners with them to identify candidates for their facilities in France, Thailand, Brazil, Mexico, and the United States. These facilities all have different cultures because their countries have different cultures. Recruiting internationally can add another layer to the importance of considering culture. When we are

---

4   Alison Konrad, *Organizational Culture, Values, and Fit in the Workplace: Making the Right Job Choices* (Ontario, Canada: Ivey Publishing, 2011).

talking to the hiring leaders in Thailand, they may be quite specific about the type of person who will be a good fit for their organization and, conversely, the type who will not. And within that single company, a candidate might be a wonderful fit for the culture in the United States and a bad fit for the culture in France or Brazil.

The secret to uncovering information about fit is in asking questions. We ask our clients to complete intake forms, but then we want to dig a little deeper, to get beyond the cut-and-paste responses on which busy hiring managers often rely. We ask things like: What's your management style? How will you work with this new candidate? What will be seen as a success in this role?

The secret to uncovering information about fit is in asking questions.

In having these kinds of conversations, we can uncover whether and how vision will impact our client's hiring decisions. I'm not focused on whether these answers are consistent with what appears in their promotional material, in their commercials, and on their website—they usually are. I'm focused on what matters to the individual hiring leader and on identifying the right people who will be a great fit.

Kelly Renz of Novo Group emphasizes that this customized approach to recruitment is especially critical when filling a CEO role. She described to me the challenge of identifying a new CEO for one of her clients, a multimillion-dollar, family-owned manufacturing company. For three generations, family members had served as CEO, but after nearly ninety years, the company had decided to hire their first professional CEO from outside the family. This company was located in a rural area, and the new CEO would need to relocate to a small town. Lastly, there was not a traditional compensation package (no stock), since the family intended to maintain their ownership of the company. The CEO's mandate was to grow the company, not prepare it for eventual sale.

Kelly's recruitment strategy was brilliant. "Using a combination of search criteria," she explained, "we targeted the academic and career geographic relocation patterns of industry executives. We were able to find six candidates to present. Each candidate had ties back to the general region, which we knew was going to be one of the key factors to find someone willing to relocate."

DISCUSSING DIVERSITY

I want to pause for a moment and talk about another hot-button issue in recruiting and in the corporate world as a whole: diversity.

It's a fact that, for too long, senior management and executives have looked the same and have followed similar paths to higher-level positions. They may even have earned degrees from the same colleges and universities and received training from the same companies.

The good news is that we are getting better at assessing people's skills and abilities in a more holistic way, and as a result, many organizations are moving in a direction that is more welcoming to managers and leaders of different genders, races, and educational backgrounds. I am enthusiastic about this movement and want to do everything I can to support it.

As part of this effort, I cochair the 2020 Phoenix Conversation on Board Diversity, a global initiative toward accelerating gender balance on corporate boards of directors. Our goal has been to raise awareness of the benefits that gender diversity brings to boardrooms. As I have conversations with leaders at organizations, I find it's an issue that matters to them—they do want to have more diversity and more women on their boards.

Some states are even passing legislation to demand more diverse corporate boards. California, for example, enacted laws in 2019 designed to ensure more representative boards by requiring that any public company that had its executive base in California must have at least one woman on its board; by 2021, the law stated, those numbers must increase, depending on the size of the board, with a goal of 20 percent representation of women. New York has passed legislation requiring foreign and domestic corporations to report the number of directors appointed to their board and to specify how many of those directors are women. This law applies to any company authorized to do business in the state, whether publicly traded or privately held.[5]

Other states have passed or are considering similar legislation—states like Colorado, Illinois, Maryland, Pennsylvania, Massachusetts, Michigan, Ohio, and New Jersey. This is a sign that diversity is a hot topic for corporate boards and that it is likely to continue to be significant in the years ahead.

And it's not just a focus for boards. Increasingly, organizations are addressing the fact that their leadership—and their employees—must reflect the population as a whole. The same is true for many of my clients. They want a more representative workforce. But the question is: How do they get there?

When clients express an interest in having a talent pool with more diverse candidates, we spend time talking to them about what that means. We want to understand their goals. We may need to have a frank conversation about why it will be more challenging for them to attract diverse individuals, whether it's their organization's mission, its location, or some other factor.

---

5   Teri Wilford Wood and Anna Broccolo, "New York Enacts Legislation Related to Board Diversity," *The National Law Review*, January 17, 2020, https://www. natlawreview.com/article/new-york-enacts-legislation-related-to-board-diversity.

It's also important to remember that the very meaning of *diversity* in human resources can be ... well, diverse. Diversity can reflect different factors, depending on the organization and its culture. A longtime family business may express an interest in adding diversity to their workforce and simply mean hiring talented people who are not family members. For other organizations, it may mean including more women, more people of color, or more individuals of different ages or educational backgrounds. We can't use a cookie-cutter approach for this type of recruiting.

Let's consider one of our clients—a higher education institution in Rhode Island that specifically requested a diverse slate of candidates for a senior-level administrative opportunity. Our first step was to discuss with them what precisely they meant. Were they interested in attracting more candidates who were women? People of color? Candidates from different types of colleges? Candidates from outside Rhode Island?

The conversation revealed that they felt that they lacked administrative leaders who reflected the racial background of many of their students, and this lack of diversity was an area they were eager to address in their recruitment search. Our solution was to target passive candidates at historically black colleges and universities (HBCs); it was a successful way to present an opportunity to qualified candidates who might not have considered a position in Rhode Island and to ensure that our client had access to an exceptional talent pool that also addressed the school's desire to demonstrate a commitment to diversity in its hiring practices.

Our goal is to always present our clients with a diverse slate of candidates. For us, that means candidates who are different from each other, because we want our client to have options. We try different approaches, tweaking our search, being willing to try a wide range of strategies to deliver that full spectrum of qualified people. There may be candidates with less experience who are at a lower salary point, candidates in the middle, and candidates on the higher end.

This is yet another way in which we partner with our clients. We understand that sometimes you don't know exactly who the ideal candidate will be, you don't know precisely who you are looking for, until you are talking with that person. Sometimes you don't know who you want until you begin the interview process. You may think that you need someone with a PhD until you talk to a candidate who has all the right skills and passion earned on the job, not through academic study. You may want to pay a lower salary but then find a candidate so good that they fully deserve the extra dollars they are expecting.

I did some follow up with a client recently who hired us to support their recruitment campaign targeting female candidates for an IT manager search. It was a challenging search, but in the end, we identified several qualified women, and they narrowed the search to a female candidate we had identified and a male candidate who they had sourced internally. They chose to hire the male candidate.

A traditional recruiter might get frustrated when that happens. But I view it as a demonstration of why recruitment research adds value to every search, even when it results in an internal hire or referral. Our clients gain valuable data from the searches we do. Every search provides an opportunity for education. Our clients are able to assess internal and external candidates and choose the individual who they feel is best qualified for the job. In this case, we were able to share with the client data about the challenges we encountered in identifying female candidates for their opportunity, and that's data that they can use to inform future hiring needs and to move forward in different directions.

WHO ARE THE "RIGHT PEOPLE" FOR YOU?

I hope that this chapter has inspired you to think more expansively about your own workforce and how recruiting decisions can shape your organization's ability to reach a broader customer base. What steps can you take today that will ensure that you are talking to the people who will add value to your organization, support your mission, and help achieve your goals?

Let's consider the big-picture legislation that we discussed earlier, in which states are requiring companies to have more representative corporate boards. This is a great goal, but it doesn't happen in isolation. If your goal is diversity on your board, among your senior executives, or in your management team, you should look first at your hiring practices for all employees. Your workforce is a community; are you cultivating a community that is diverse? If your workforce is almost all white men, your leadership is unlikely to look very different.

With recruitment research, our focus is not simply on the immediate hiring need but on equipping our clients to build a talent pipeline. That should be your goal, too. It can be challenging when your network is made up of people who all look very much the same, who share a background or a race or a gender.

But I encourage you to be proactive and to take actions now to build that network before you have a specific hiring need. Think about the kinds of people you'd like to see as part of your team, or in your organization, or on your board. Do you want to add women to your leadership team? Are you eager to have more people of color serve on your board? Do you require administrators who can better speak to the needs of people of diverse genders, or sexual orientations, or economic backgrounds? Is your goal to include more people from a specific industry or who have a background in human resources or finance or marketing?

If you're struggling with the process, hire a recruitment research firm like ours to make those introductions. Start with a goal of making those connections so that, when an opportunity arises to fill a seat on the board or to hire a new CEO, those conversations can expand to a more active discussion of specific opportunities.

Begin that conversation now. Expand your community and build relationships with different people. Don't settle for a network that looks and thinks like you. Make sure that you truly are talking to the right people.

ACTION PLAN

- Identify three key elements of your corporate culture that will impact hiring decisions.

- Assess your organization's diversity—do the board and senior management represent your workforce? Your customers?

- Instead of job descriptions, create a strategic resource that spells out precisely what success looks like in each role in your organization.

CHAPTER SEVEN

MAKE A LIST OF CANDIDATES

Until now, we've focused on the opportunities and benefits that recruitment research offers to you as a hiring leader. But let's shift perspectives for just a brief moment and consider our process from the point of view of the ideal candidate—the person who is exactly the kind of employee you'd love to add to your organization.

Imagine that you are sitting in your office, preparing to begin yet another busy day. You've been with your current employer for five years and have been a key player in a recent successful new product introduction or in solving a tricky problem that has hindered the organization's ability to enter a new market. Your performance reviews have all been excellent. You are proud of what you've accomplished and are respected by others in your division.

The phone rings. It is a recruiter, and she is eager to talk to you about an opportunity at another organization.

What is your first response? You are probably flattered—it's wonderful to be recognized and sought after for your accomplishments. But think for a moment about what comes next. What should that recruiter say to spark your interest? What could she say to make you consider a new opportunity?

This is the challenge I face as a recruiter. I need to craft the right message, one that will effectively communicate the opportunity my client is offering in a way that will excite and intrigue the right candidate. It's a bit of psychology and a bit of branding all wrapped up in one often brief initial conversation.

Recruitment research plays a critical role in that preliminary contact. By the time I make that first cold call, I want to have the information at my fingertips that will persuade potential candidates that this opportunity is the right one for them. The first call matters; it gives me an opportunity to perform an initial vetting, getting a sense of the candidate's personality while also providing a chance to confirm their credentials.

A PERFECT PITCH

I wish that there was a template for these cold calls—a script to follow that would ensure that every candidate we speak with is instantly excited about the opportunity and fully qualified for the job. That script would be incredibly valuable! But I suppose it would also make the work I do less interesting and rewarding.

I mentioned earlier that my favorite part of the recruiting process is learning about the sizzle—the special and unique factors that an organization has that will spark the interest of potential candidates. It's wonderful to help my clients identify their sizzle, but the payoff comes when I can use that unique factor to tell their story to potential candidates. This means that every pitch must be unique.

These initial conversations are important for generating potential candidates, but they are also a valuable source of data for us and for our clients. It's not until we start having conversations with potential candidates that we can get a true assessment of the status of our search. These early conversations reveal whether we've developed a large enough target list. If, after a few conversations, we realize that we're not reaching the right candidates, we know that we may need to spend more time researching companies, since the position is so specific or the skill set is so narrow that we need to add more companies or industries to our search.

We can also gauge the success of our research based on the level of interest from candidates. If the right people are excited by the opportunity we're describing, we can feel confident that we will be able to provide our client with a strong list of candidates. If not, if we hear a lot of objections about our client from potential candidates or a lack of interest in the opportunity, we need to work with our client to develop a new strategy to ensure that they can access the talent they need.

Although I described this initial contact as a *cold call*, I should note that our first contact is not always a telephone call. We know that some people prefer to be approached by email. Generally speaking, that's true of engineers and technical people. On the other hand, if we're recruiting for sales positions or for people doing development in the higher education world, those are people who are more social, who are comfortable having lots of conversations with different people and networking using different platforms. Those are the people whom we approach first with a phone call.

The goal in that first call is to share just enough information to spark their interest. We don't want to overwhelm a candidate with too many details about the opportunity. We just want to start a conversation—one that we hope they'll be eager to continue.

Often we don't speak with the candidate directly on that first approach. We have to leave a message on their voice mail that is informative enough, intriguing enough, that they just have to call us back.

To give you a glimpse of what that message sounds like from the perspective of our target candidate, let me share the script from one call, this by a Duffy Group practice leader with expertise in higher education.

Imagine that you are a talented professional working in university development and you discover this message in your voice mail:

"I'm an executive recruiter and I'm reaching out to you regarding an exciting search we're conducting for a highly regarded institution. Our client is a top-tier university in *US News and World Reports* rankings. They have a newly created role of managing director of development for their College of Business, and it's a great opportunity for many reasons. The culture for the College of Business is student-centered. The faculty is very involved with the students. They have a high retention rate and impressive graduation rates. It's very entrepreneurial. The College of Business makes their own money. They're good at it. This person can build their own shop and help them grow. The dean is a dynamic leader who has put them on a great trajectory. She exudes integrity. Their values are at the forefront of what they do. They offer excellent programs and have hardworking people. They just finished a successful campaign. The president is very advancement-focused, and the location is a desirable place to live. I'd welcome a chance to talk with you further."

It's a great message, isn't it? In just a few minutes, you've learned several key factors. First, the opportunity is with a well-known university. From a development perspective, it's important that people recognize the university's name and respect its reputation. Next, she's stated that the role for which she's recruiting is newly created. There isn't a dusty framework to follow of how things need to be done in that role, and you aren't replacing a well-loved, longtime member of the team. There's an opportunity to shape the role in a unique way.

There's also important information about the dean—presumably the person to whom this candidate would be reporting. It's a woman, integrity matters to her, she's focused on advancement, and the university has recently concluded a successful campaign, suggesting that there are key pieces already in place that will support any new development efforts. Plus, as a bit of icing on the cake, there's the detail that this job is in a place where candidates will be excited to relocate.

What would your response be to that call? Wouldn't you at least want to follow up, to get a bit more information about the opportunity?

For the candidate our practice leader was targeting with this pitch, the answer was yes.

"He told me that he gets a lot of calls," she said, "and he never returns them. But this opportunity sounded so interesting, he needed to learn more about it."

GETTING TO YES

Our goal in these conversations is to get potential candidates engaged. We want to promote our client and the opportunity they are offering. We want to confirm that the candidate has the right skills and training. And we want to gauge their level of interest.

Usually, the first message, that initial contact, is simply an introduction. It leads to a longer, detailed conversation in which we can share additional information and learn more about the potential candidate. Understandably, many candidates prefer to schedule these conversations when they aren't at work, often at a time before or after their office hours.

Even when those initial conversations are brief, there are a few things we look for, signs that we are on the right track. Of course, a positive sign is when the potential candidate immediately expresses interest in being considered. It's also a great sign when they indicate that they are familiar with our client. Once in a while, we even hear something like "Wow! That's a company I've always wanted to work for." As you can imagine, that's a phrase that makes recruiters very happy.

Sometimes the location helps sell the opportunity. We do a lot of recruiting for clients in Colorado. Even when candidates aren't interested in relocating, they may be willing to reconsider when we tell them that the opportunity is in Colorado. I'm based in Arizona; its warm, dry weather can be a draw for candidates starved for sunshine.

But not every conversation is easy. Sometimes those conversations reveal that our client has a recruiting challenge, something we'll want to address as part of our strategy session so that we can better promote the position and the opportunity to potential candidates.

Let me give you an example of this kind of challenge. One of our clients is a New England-based organization, a family-owned business successfully operating for four generations. The longtime CEO was highly respected in the industry, but several years ago, he decided to step back from running the business and a new CEO was hired. That individual was not a good fit; he engaged in some questionable deals, and during his tenure, the company's reputation was damaged. Ultimately, that individual was fired and the family persuaded the former CEO to step back into his role.

When we recruit for this company, it's important that we tell candidates that the organization has cleaned house. We want them to know that the original CEO is back in his role and that the business has taken decisive steps to eliminate any dysfunction caused during that brief period.

TELLING THE STORY

A key part of recruiting is telling the story—or, more specifically, telling our client's story. My goal is to frame an opportunity in a way that will get candidates excited and eager to learn more. I have to be able to explain why a candidate would want to leave a place where they may be quite happy and go to work for someone else.

Let's be honest—it's not easy to leave a job. It's not easy to sever relationships and give up earned status or seniority. For many people, there's comfort in the familiarity of known relationships and a routine commute. It's even more challenging if a relocation is involved, requiring a candidate to sell their home, or give up an apartment, and move to a different part of the country.

I need to be able to answer the question "Why?" What is it about this opportunity that makes all that change and challenge worthwhile? What factors will more than compensate for the inconvenience and the disruption?

If the candidate responds with a certain level of enthusiasm to our first contact, I can feel a lot more confident that they may be able to partially answer that question themselves. But if not, I acknowledge their loyalty to their current employer. After all, that loyalty is a great trait and is even more evidence that they may be an excellent addition to my client's organization.

I use a key phrase with candidates, one that's designed to highlight the opportunity without disparaging their current employer.

I tell them that my client is doing *something different*.

Why does this phrase work so effectively? For potential candidates who are happy in their job, who haven't considered leaving, it doesn't disparage their current employer. There's no criticism in their decision to be a part of their current organization. It doesn't impose values, suggesting that one business is better than another.

It simply says that my client is doing things ... *differently*.

Most people are naturally curious. Let's say that you are a skilled hospital administrator, successfully managing a large staff, delivering exceptional patient care, and overseeing a multimillion-dollar budget. Even if you are quite happy with your current role and your employer, you are probably interested in discovering how another healthcare organization is doing things differently. What exactly does that mean? And what can you learn from their approach?

This is why the sizzle I talked about earlier is so critical. Every successful business, every successful organization, must be able to identify what it is that is special and unique, the factor that distinguishes them from their competitors. It is the single most crucial thing you can do to dramatically improve your ability to attract the best people to your company.

There is no specific rubric of success when it comes to telling the story. Because each opportunity is unique, I can't give you a formula to use to gauge the effectiveness of our strategy. I can't say, for instance, that a successful pitch translates into 30 percent or more of the candidates we approach expressing interest.

But recruitment research is built on data, and we can judge progress based on our update reports. If we see that a recruiter hasn't received a lot of returned calls or emails from potential candidates, if there's not a lot of engagement, then it's clear that our strategy needs to be examined. Possibly the pitch needs to be tweaked, maybe candidates who are being called should be targeted by email or vice versa. We are always thinking strategically about our approach and revising it to ensure that we get a better result.

Successful recruiting isn't rocket science, but it requires quick thinking and excellent analytical skills. Our strategy needs to evolve, depending on the initial results. We have to be thoughtful to ensure that our approach reflects the client and the opportunity. And we need to be nimble to assess each candidate and to tailor our pitch to that specific individual. If we're pitching one hundred potential candidates, that same pitch may be tweaked one hundred times, based on the knowledge that an opportunity may need to be framed differently to a candidate in Chicago in January and a candidate in Arizona in July. We need to be smart, and we need to be strategic.

> **Successful recruiting isn't rocket science, but it requires quick thinking and excellent analytical skills.**

PERSISTENCE AND PROGRESS

Clients frequently want to know how many times we'll approach a potential candidate, how many conversations it takes to qualify them. The answer: it takes as many as it takes.

For some candidates, we may have two conversations before they express interest in the opportunity. For others, it may take three or four approaches.

We understand that it takes time to promote an opportunity effectively. It also takes time to do the hard work of screening candidates to make sure that they are fully qualified.

We may initially approach some candidates by email, but we want to make sure to always have a conversation, either by phone or video chat. We would never present a candidate to a client without speaking with them, without having that conversation.

There is, of course, valuable data that you can gather just by looking at someone's résumé or work history. If a candidate has been with an employer for five or more years, it's likely that they are performing or they wouldn't still be there. If they have risen steadily in their career, progressing in seniority, you can be confident that they are doing something right. Conversely, if you see someone changing jobs frequently, or large gaps in their work history, they may not be red flags, but they are certainly something you would want to address before determining whether they'd be a good fit.

Three to five people. That's the goal. When I present a list of candidates to my client, I want to have three to five names on that list.

Sometimes a position is so specific and requires such a unique skill set that there may only be a handful of people in the world who are qualified. Then, that list may be smaller.

Sometimes a client has requested a strategy that isn't generating the kinds of candidates they want—they may not be offering a high enough salary, or they may only be considering candidates from a specific region or with a specific degree or some other framework that is creating barriers to our search. This informs our strategy and plays a role in the market data we generate. We'll talk more about that in the next chapter.

But always, we want to be able to generate the right candidates for the opportunity by telling our client's story.

The skills I've developed as a recruiter translate to many different areas, both professionally and personally. I'm a wonderful guest at cocktail parties! I can easily talk to lots of different people about what they do for a living and have a very rich conversation based on my knowledge of many different industries. I relish those kinds of interactions and deeper dialogues.

But you don't have to be an expert at recruiting—or at social conversation—to employ some of the key strategies I've discussed in this chapter. Reflect on your organization's branding, not only to outsiders or to clients but also to employees and potential employees. What is the story that you want to tell? What is it that you are doing differently? Your answers to these questions will equip you to promote opportunities and to build a much more effective—and engaged—workforce.

ACTION PLAN

- Identify three factors that are unique to your organization—three things that you are doing differently from your competitors.

- Consider your organization's current branding efforts: Which messages will be especially effective at attracting great employees?

- Assess your organization's story; analyze any changes that point out messaging inconsistencies when your audience shifts from potential clients to employees to board members.

CHAPTER EIGHT

CAPTURE THE MARKET DATA

One of the reasons I'm such a passionate advocate for recruitment research is the value we deliver to clients.

That value isn't simply a list of names.

It's the market data.

When we partner with clients on a search, delivering a slate of qualified candidates is only one goal. We want to help our clients move beyond filling an immediate vacancy to equipping them to build a talent pipeline that will support future opportunities.

The key to this is market data—the rich trove of information we've uncovered throughout our research. In any search, we identify many candidates before we build our short list of only those individuals who are highly qualified for a specific opportunity. We may screen one hundred people before reaching a short list of three to five. And although the candidates who didn't make the short list may not be the best fit for one specific opportunity, they may be perfect for a future need with our client's organization.

That's why our market research includes a database of candidates—we call it a *talent database* and give it to the client at the end of the assignment. It provides names and résumés that can be used for future searches. This underscores the value of recruitment research and our practice of using billable hours. Our client has paid us to uncover a broad list of names before we arrive at our final short list. They should have access to all our research results, not simply a short list of candidate names. We understand that business needs change; today's investment in recruitment research will continue to pay rewards well into the future for our clients.

There are times when we've uncovered candidates who we just know will be a good fit for our client's organization. Their skills and background may not be a perfect match for this specific opportunity, but there's an element of matchmaking in good recruiting, and there are times when you sense that an individual and your client should be introduced.

We make that introduction. We call these kinds of candidates *outliers*. They may be a bit atypical from the others we're presenting, but when we have that sense, we always include them on our list. Often our clients end up hiring them for other opportunities.

Because we're using this unique model of recruitment research, we can help our clients in this way by supporting their efforts to build a talent pipeline. We don't charge them more money for generating these additional candidates. Recruitment research enables us to shift our focus from responding to specific tasks to doing what's best for our client.

Our market data also includes competitive intelligence that we've uncovered during our search. What does this mean? We may discover valuable information about salaries or benefits our client's competitors are offering. We may gain insight into our client's reputation in their industry or learn of new businesses that may present a challenge to their competitive advantage.

The goal, of course, is to make sure that we're not simply supplying our clients with facts and figures. Too often, businesses are inundated with data, leading to an unsatisfactory situation in which they can be data rich and yet still information poor.

John Ladley and Thomas C. Redman are strategic thinkers who have developed practices to ensure that organizations better manage the data they receive. They propose that businesses develop data scenarios—they call them *value modes*—and use them to organize data into specific strategic priorities.[6]

This is an intriguing approach and one that aligns with our method of using recruitment research. Our reports aren't simply a list of names and contact information; we include data that can improve our client's understanding of what their competitors are doing and paying.

> **Too often, businesses are inundated with data, leading to an unsatisfactory situation in which they can be data rich and yet still information poor.**

---

6   John Ladley and Thomas C. Redman, "Use Data to Accelerate Your Business Strategy," *Harvard Business Review*, March 3, 2020, https://hbr.org/2020/03/use-data-to-accelerate-your-business-strategy.

DOES YOUR BUDGET ALIGN WITH YOUR GOALS?

Among the most valuable data we provide our clients is feedback on the candidate's compensation. When we talk with passive candidates, we tell our client's story, we talk about what they are doing differently, we promote the opportunity. There are many factors that excite potential candidates and that lead to an ongoing conversation.

But let's be honest: salary matters. One study showed that the most important factor impacting a candidate's decision to accept a new job was the compensation; nearly half of those surveyed said that it influenced their decision more than any other factor.[7]

Practice leader Colleen Neese says that compensation information is the most valuable data we provide clients as part of our market research. "It helps with every search that I'm working on," she explained. "I see how it helps even with the selling process, because many of our clients know that they have a position to fill, but typically one of their biggest challenges is where they should be in terms of compensation to be competitive yet not break their budget. Collecting and sharing that compensation information throughout our recruitment process is extremely helpful."

Our market research data helps clients understand the impact of their budget and reveals to them how the compensation package they are offering may or may not reflect market realities. Duffy Group's Eden Higgins likens this to the HGTV show *Property Brothers*.

---

7   Michael Schneider, "7 LinkedIn Statistics That Will Make You Question Your Recruitment Strategy," *Inc.*, June 14, 2018, https://www.inc.com/michael-schneider/7-linkedin-hiring-trends-that-will-change-way-you-recruit.html.

"At the start of the episode," Eden said, "they may be working with a couple with a two-hundred-fifty-thousand-dollar budget. And they'll show that couple a beautiful house that has everything on their wish list—a gorgeous kitchen, a huge master suite, all the upgrades. And the couple gets very excited and says, 'Oh, this is perfect! This is a great house! It has everything we want!' And then they reveal the fact that the house doesn't cost two hundred fifty thousand dollars. It costs five hundred thousand dollars."

Eden explains that some of her clients may start their search with similarly unrealistic expectations—with champagne taste and a grape juice budget. In the initial intake discussion, they may state that they only want to interview candidates with an MBA or PhD or a very specific set of qualifications, and yet they only want to pay half of what these types of candidates typically receive. She may identify a very qualified candidate—one who is interested—but who lacks that desired PhD.

This is where the market data can inform the client's search. First, the report can reflect the results of our search, especially when candidates are qualified and interested, yet the client chooses not to move forward with them because they lack a particular degree. Next, it can educate clients to the realities of the market—that the candidate they love, with the résumé that they've placed at the top of their list, is commanding a much higher salary than they planned to offer.

Eden explains that she puts that résumé on Duffy Group letter-head if the candidate is interested with a note that she realizes that they are out of the price range. "I want them [the client] to under-stand that this is what you have to pay if you want that candidate who is the equivalent of the five-hundred-thousand-dollar house. That's what you have to pay to get everything on your wish list. And they can then compare it with the candidates who are within their price point and decide whether they want to reassess the compensation they are offering."

We share the compensation requirements for all the candidates we talk to as well as all the candidates we present to a client. The client can see any trends; it shows them what they should be paying to attract candidates with specific qualifications. It gives them valuable insight so that they can see the candidates they will draw for a fixed amount of money as well as the candidates who will become interested if they increase their compensation in certain specific ways (which, of course, we spell out). That compensation data can help them determine whether they are going to reach the candidates they need for a particular role.

Amanda Piriano of Thorn Network notes the importance of this data in helping clients achieve their recruiting goals. "A national Fortune 500 company came to Thorn looking for help," she explained. "The company really wanted competitor talent, so that is where our search began. When we talked with this talent, we found out that our client's salary range was not enough to attract them, so we used this data to influence them to look outside the industry. With this change in strategic direction, we were able to find highly qualified candidates within similar industries and the client hired from that new strategy. With this success, we earned their trust and business. We have now been supporting them for over two years and have filled several roles for them. In fact, the head of real estate for this company has instructed his entire team to only use us if they ever go outside due to our creative thinking and success."

Sometimes clients need to operate within their stated budget. Sometimes they choose to increase their compensation package.

Regardless of their decision, the market data we provide has educated them to market realities and can be used to inform future hiring decisions.

This kind of data is particularly valuable for the hard-to-source candidates, those who are specialists or who are filling a very niche role. One of our clients is a pharmaceutical company; they hired us to identify candidates with clinical development experience and who had performed research in the specific area they were focusing on for drug development. They wanted candidates with industry experience rather than academic research experience.

As you can imagine, this was a very targeted search. The market data we collected showed them—as Eden might put it—the equivalent of the $500,000 house. We could use our market research to clarify for them precisely who the candidates were who met their strict criteria and detail where they were working and what compensation they were receiving in their current position. The search resulted in two highly qualified candidates in the pipeline and a client who is fully informed on exactly what the market realities are for that position in that market.

KNOWLEDGE IS POWER

The market data we provide to clients not only supports their competitive advantage; it's also our competitive advantage. It is yet another key area in which recruitment research differs from traditional recruiting methods.

Sheila Greco of SGA Talent says that her clients find great value in the research her firm shares on the talent pool—the statistics and data. "We are always doing data analytics behind the talent pool," she told me, "and that includes diversity and inclusion. We share all our notes with them [the clients]." Her clients may get multiple hires from that single talent pool as a result of examining the data and seeing the different types of talent their competitors have.

The hiring managers with whom Sheila works will often share the research with their company's talent management team, especially their competitors' organizational chart. This prompts helpful questions: How are we unique? How are we different? What do we need to change? Do we have as much diversity as our competitors?

"What sets us apart," Sheila explained, "is that we give them this information. We're not afraid to because we're all about being a true partner."

Too often, recruiters—especially recruiters who specialize in a particular area or industry—want to preserve working relationships with competing businesses. As a result, they are unlikely to provide one organization with information about its competition.

Our focus is not on potential future clients; our focus is on our existing client and on providing them with the research we uncover during our search. That means informing our clients about their competitors' organizational structure, which companies are hiring or firing, which are restructuring, and of course what they are paying employees and the benefits they're offering.

Traditional recruiters are filling a legitimate role—providing clients with a slate of candidates for a specific job as quickly as possible. Their goal is to deliver a candidate who is going to be hired.

For some clients, that approach makes sense. But for our clients, the market data—the competitive intelligence—is extremely valuable. It can change the direction of their recruitment campaign and equip them to meet future staffing challenges.

Duffy Group's Melissa Barker explains that the market data can be particularly helpful for smaller clients. "I've been on several calls recently with smaller clients who say, 'I feel like I'm on an island and I don't really understand what else is out there,'" she said. "They look to us to partner with them to help them fully understand the marketplace: how much competitors are paying, what their benefits look like, what the candidates who are looking for a position right now really want beyond salary. What are their nonnegotiables? Our goal is to provide a broader picture of their industry, of that particular position, both regionally and locally. We provide that feedback in real time, on a weekly basis, on their update reports so they can clearly understand what it is that we're finding."

Sharon Grace is a practice leader who spent nearly two decades in traditional recruiting before joining my company and becoming a strong advocate for the recruitment research method. A recent search in which she worked closely with the hiring manager illustrates the value of the market data we provide. The position was newly created and the client—a university in Colorado—had never worked with an outside recruiter before. I'll let Sharon pick up the story.

"The position involved working remotely in the Denver area. It's a role that requires skill in sales and fundraising. Because the school focuses on energy management, the ideal candidate needed to be comfortable working with CEOs and senior managers in the oil and gas industries as well as solar. Oil and gas are big industries in Colorado, but solar is also very important—and they all have political connotations. But the role also involved student recruitment, so the candidate needed to be skilled at talking to high school students.

"I sensed that the salary they planned to offer might be a little low, and Colorado is a state where we're unable to directly ask candidates what their compensation is. So we needed to dig deeper to see what we could uncover.

"I had several calls with the client to discuss their concerns. They really wanted more data to better understand their landscape—data that supplied the details they were trying to capture and to help them develop a strategy. Our goal was to gather a lot of information to help them hone in on the best candidate."

Compensation is one piece of this, but other data we provide also supports strategic planning. Our nonprofit clients need data that helps them understand and interpret trends in funding and budgets. Some of our nonprofit clients receive their support in specific percentages—say, 90 percent from the government and 10 percent through philanthropic donations and fundraising. That can be a challenging and unpredictable ratio—government funding can be scaled back or eliminated altogether. For those clients, it can be quite helpful to learn that other nonprofits operating in their space are working to shift toward a sixty/forty split between government support and fundraising. It opens their eyes to the kinds of changes they may need to make to ensure more stable support for their organization.

These observations are all illustrations of why market data matters. When you're dealing with hard-to-fill positions, when you're operating in a competitive environment, when you need to have a clear picture of the factors impacting hiring strategies or budgets or fundraising, knowledge is power.

ACTION PLAN

- Analyze the nonnegotiables for recent hires in your organization. What patterns do you see?

- Assess your competitors. Who is hiring? Who is firing? Who is restructuring?

- Look beyond your landscape. If you operate locally, gather regional or national data to compare your compensation packages with those that candidates might find elsewhere.

CHAPTER NINE

INTERVIEWING CANDIDATES

I t's obvious to anyone who spends a few minutes with me: I love meeting people. When I meet you, I want to know your story and find out a bit about your background and the things you're passionate about. It's one reason why recruiting is my business— a business that brings me joy. There are countless opportunities to connect with people and to learn about their professional life.

The interview process is one opportunity to have those kinds of conversations. Yet I'm surprised by how many candidates dread them and how many clients find them almost as stressful as the candidates.

If you're an executive or hiring manager who shares this perspective on interviewing, let me reassure you. The interview is an important part of your fact-finding mission, but it should be part of a broader strategy and consist of more than a single conversation. In this chapter, I want to share our approach to interviewing candidates, one based on the key concepts of recruitment research.

DOING A DEEP DIVE

Earlier in the book, I explained how we promote opportunities to candidates. As I noted, we expect to have more than one conversation with a candidate to discuss the position, share key facts about our client, and confirm that they have the skills and experience necessary to be a strong applicant. This process can take anywhere from two to four conversations with a candidate before they've expressed clear interest and we feel confident that they belong on the list we're presenting to our client.

We call this *warm lead generation*—it's a screening interview, or series of interviews, to confirm that a candidate is interested and that they meet the qualifications of the position. Once this process is complete, we deliver the warm leads to our client. With this list, they can determine which candidates they want to interview more intensely to gain additional data about their level of experience, to determine their cultural fit, and to ascertain their motivation for taking the job.

For some clients, this initial vetting—the warm lead generation step—is the final piece that they need from us; they have the internal staff to perform more intensive follow-up interviewing. But other clients depend on us to do a more thorough evaluation of candidates in a process I call the *deep dive*.

What does this mean? The deep dive involves developing a much richer level of detail surrounding a candidate's skills and experience. It's going beyond the job description, beyond the résumé, to uncover all the factors that will confirm that a candidate is the best fit.

Let's take a look at a specific job opportunity to give you a better idea of what I mean. Imagine that you are the hiring manager who needs to identify candidates for the position of VP of contracting for your organization. The initial step, the warm lead generation, includes confirming that a candidate has contracting experience. But once you've confirmed that your candidate has fifteen years of experience, you want to go deeper and learn precisely what that experience entails.

The deep dive requires you to ask questions that are more comprehensive and more specific. You want to uncover real deliverables and accomplishments. Instead of focusing just on titles and tasks, you need to ask questions like "What are the results of what you've done?" In the case of the candidate for your VP of contracting opportunity, you'll want to know details and specific examples of contracts they've been responsible for securing. Your questions will be framed to uncover these details, asking things like "Have you done value-based contracting?"

When we perform deep-dive interviews, our goal is to give our clients the specifics that will equip them to make informed hiring decisions. Instead of saying that our VP of contracting candidate has fifteen years of contracting experience, we want to be able to show that they were responsible for a 100 percent increase in providers. These are the kinds of details that reveal precisely what those fifteen years of contracting experience translated into for their organization. The deep dive should uncover results.

For some of our clients, the deep dive also needs to focus on culture. This is particularly true for smaller organizations and family-owned businesses. When culture matters for a client, I'll be asking lots of questions designed to get a good feel for a candidate's personality. I might ask about their current and previous employers—the number of employees, the revenue, their industry. The words candidates use to describe past employment can be quite revealing. As they talk, I'm listening—listening to their responses and also to their descriptions of the work cultures they've been part of in the past. These details provide key information that is helpful in assessing cultural fit.

Melissa Barker, Duffy Group's Practice Director, uses one question with candidates when interviewing to determine cultural fit. She says that it was once requested by a client, and she's found it quite helpful.

"I ask candidates, 'Do you trust people instinctively, or do they have to earn your trust?'" She explained, "For one client, if the answer was 'They have to earn my trust,' that candidate was not a good fit for the organization. Regardless of anything else on their résumé, they were out."

This may seem strict—even severe—but for this particular client, it was a clear marker of whether a candidate would work well in their culture. "You can't coach a candidate on how to answer that question," Melissa noted. "We had some fabulous candidates who didn't make it past the initial interview stage because of their answer to that question."

Recruitment research is based on knowledge building, gathering information at each stage and using that data to inform and support the strategy for the next step. When we first talk to clients and discuss their recruitment goals during the intake meeting, we ask clients if there is anything specific they'd like us to uncover during the interview stage. For some clients, concrete industry experience is very critical. For others, they want to learn more about a candidate's technical knowledge, whether it's expertise in SAS programming or revenue recognition or any of the forms of highly specialized knowledge that a position may require.

It comes back to that idea of partnership with our client. Together, we collaborate from the beginning to develop a framework for assessing candidates and then use that framework during the interview process to confirm fit.

Certain questions may help weed out candidates whose current title may mask a lack of deep knowledge in a particular facet of their job. If I use terminology that's a marker of expertise and the candidate seems confused or asks for more details, that's a sign that they may not be the right person for this opportunity.

MOTIVATION MATTERS

Culture, knowledge, results—these are all vital pieces of the deep-dive interview. But there's one more element that can ensure that a potential candidate finds their way onto our final list—or is eliminated. That element is motivation.

As we've discussed, we dedicate time and energy to promoting opportunities to candidates. As part of our deep-dive interview, we want to find out what inspires someone who may not have been actively looking for a new job to pursue this one.

This may seem self-serving, and it is of course helpful to know which of our approaches was more effective and which was less so when discussing opportunities with passive candidates, but when we explore motivation during the deep-dive interview, we want to know *why*. Why this opportunity, at this time, for this organization. We'll ask a candidate, "What's motivating you to consider a job change?" Or "What is it about this opportunity that has piqued your interest?" The answer to those questions is very revealing and tells you something about a candidate that you won't find on their résumé.

Consider these potential different responses to the first question: "What's motivating you to consider a job change?"

- "I've always wanted to work for that organization."

- "I'm excited by the expansion plans you described and eager to contribute to that kind of growth."

- "I enjoy what I'm doing, but it's a little too easy. I want to challenge myself."

- "I appreciate the higher salary and better benefits."

- "I respect the role your client plays in their community and like their commitment to their mission."

Each of these answers is quite different. None is wrong; depending on the opportunity and the organization, one answer may suggest a better fit than another. But they all reveal motivation while giving you some valuable insight into the candidate as well.

> **Most candidates' motivation centers around three key elements: money, position, and location.**

Most candidates' motivation centers around three key elements: money, position, and location. Money is a tricky one. If a candidate indicates that they are considering a new opportunity because of the salary, it's important to recognize that they may choose to stay if their current employer matches whatever our client is offering.

So we ask other questions—questions designed to uncover more of their motivation in considering this opportunity. Are they working with other recruiters? Are there other companies that interest them? What specifically do they like and dislike about our opportunity? How does it compare to their current position?

Because we are representing our client in this deep-dive interview, we need to be able to honestly assess whether the candidate really will leave their current employer by identifying whether we are offering them something better. Sometimes we're not. We know that, and we help our client understand that as well. Candidates are human beings, emotions play a role, and people can change their minds. So we are constantly touching base with candidates throughout this process, checking in to gauge their ongoing level of interest—and to find out if anything has changed, if another recruiter has contacted them, if there have been any impactful developments at their current employer.

John Sullivan is a professor of management at San Francisco State University. He specializes in HR strategy and has written countless books and articles on talent management, recruiting strategies, and employment branding.

His rules for interview questions that result in great hires are worth sharing here. He recommends avoiding those easy-to-answer questions, the ones that most candidates have rehearsed responses to—questions like "What are your strengths and weaknesses?" and "Where would you like to be in five years?"[8] He also advises against using questions that ask candidates about how they've solved problems in the past or requiring them to describe a circumstance in which they demonstrated leadership. According to Sullivan, these kinds of "historical" questions often involve circumstances and situations that are specific to a particular organization or job culture and may involve techniques and strategies that are quickly outdated or irrelevant in their next opportunity.

---

8   John Sullivan, "7 Rules for Job Interview Questions That Result in Great Hires," *Harvard Business Review*, February 10, 2016, https://hbr.org/2016/02/7-rules-for-job-interview-questions-that-result-in-great-hires.

Sullivan recommends that hiring managers and executives focus on asking questions that determine whether candidates can solve problems and innovate. One strategy he suggests is asking candidates to solve an actual problem, one they are likely to encounter on their first day on the job. When using this question, it helps if you've prepared in advance a list of the typical steps they'll need to follow. Then you can track their responses, seeing if they have ticked off the recommended parts of the process—or brought a new approach to the kinds of problems they'll typically encounter.

Finally, Sullivan emphasizes the importance of seeking out candidates who are forward-looking. He recommends asking a candidate to anticipate ways in which their job is likely to change in the next three to five years and to brainstorm ways that firms should evolve to respond to these potential changes.

Every interviewer should develop questions that suit their specific industry—and, of course, the opportunity. Some positions require greater innovation, some rely heavily on skilled leadership, and others demand the ability to network and increase revenue. But motivated employees are a key to every successful organization, so a wise interviewer assesses motivation before an offer of employment is extended.

THE DEEP DIVE IN ACTION

Recruitment research's customization means that each search is unique. We are able to do strategic deep-dive interviews because we've become experts at our client's business and the specific needs of the position they want to fill.

As a result, we can achieve a kind of seamless partnership so that the candidates we're interviewing may not distinguish between us and their prospective employer. Our goal is to be that extension of our client's human resources team, freeing them up to focus on other critical areas.

Let me share one story that illustrates this partnership. It involves one of our clients—a respected medical center—that was undergoing a significant expansion. In the past, they had depended on their skilled HR team to handle all aspects of hiring, including posting jobs, evaluating applicants, and then managing the administrative pieces of onboarding staff. But this particular expansion was governed by a contract that required a quick completion of the deliverables—specifically, the hiring of more than fifty new full-time staff members.

This kind of rapid scaling up would be challenging for any organization to manage. The ability to outsource the recruitment to us—to rely on our expertise at identifying qualified candidates and conducting interviews—meant that our client's HR team could focus on critical training and development. Within forty-five days, our client had fifty-three new employees, meeting their contractual obligation. In addition, our research into compensation ensured that our client's offers were competitive while allowing their team the time and resources to integrate these new hires into a successfully expanded medical center.

This is a reminder of how recruitment research saves our clients time—time that they can spend on areas that will enhance their organization's effectiveness and growth. When I'm talking about the benefits of this method, I often tell potential clients, "There are only so many hours in the day, and you're juggling a lot of balls. Wouldn't it be nice if you only had to focus on three to five candidates for this key position and get them over the finish line?"

Clients respond to that concept, and I understand why. Getting candidates over the finish line is the fun part, the exciting piece, the stage where you're talking with and assessing several highly qualified candidates and determining which one is the best fit for your needs and your organization. It's much more interesting to stand at the finish line and see the best of the best excel.

We all know that time is money. When you have a key role that's gone unfilled for three months, or six, or even nine, that's a lot of lost revenue impacting your organization.

The value of recruitment research is clear in this equation. If you can see candidates in a month or less—if, within thirty days, you can have qualified candidates who you can begin interviewing—you've saved both time and revenue. If the net result is that, within sixty days, or ninety days for particularly hard-to-fill niche positions, you'll be extending an offer of employment, you're not spending nine months vetting candidates. And you've filled a key position, you're equipping your organization to focus resources in other areas.

I believe in my clients. I believe in their story. I believe in the work they do. And that enthusiasm translates into a determination to help connect them with the right people who can help them grow and continue to do the great work they're doing.

ACTION PLAN

- Prepare for future hiring needs by incorporating key deliverables into each job description in your organization.

- Include at least one question in your interview process that will equip you to better understand a candidate's motivation for pursuing this opportunity.

- Identify the skills that are most critical for each unique opportunity—teamwork, leadership, problem-solving, innovative thinking—and then create interview questions that will enable you to measure these skills in potential candidates.

CHAPTER TEN

THINKING INSIDE AND OUTSIDE THE BOX

When it comes to the best candidate for our clients, we are agnostic.

We understand that sometimes you need to search outside your organization for your next great hire. And sometimes the perfect candidate happens to be someone who is already a part of your organization.

With the traditional recruiting approach, it's difficult to make this kind of apples-to-apples comparison. Traditional recruiters generally base their fees on successfully identifying an external hire, with a percentage of the candidate's total compensation as the recruiter's compensation. Their focus will be on quickly and efficiently identifying external candidates for the opportunity.

But the recruitment research approach enables us to use a different strategy to support your hiring needs. Our focus is on identifying the best candidate for your opportunity, whether that means an external candidate or an internal candidate.

That's why I say that we are agnostic. We are happy to ensure that your internal candidates receive the same thorough vetting as any external passive candidates we uncover during a search. In fact, we insist on treating all candidates for a position the same, using the same assessments and evaluations to ensure that we truly are presenting the best of the best to our clients. Our billing structure equips us to perform the same rigorous vetting on all candidates so that our final list isn't shaped or influenced by the candidates who will bring us more money.

Nearly every search that we perform includes internal candidates. We encourage our clients to consider internal candidates and to use our expertise to vet them against external candidates. And when internal candidates are presented to us, we clarify for them up front that our interview process will be the same for all candidates so that they understand that our recommendations are going to be completely neutral.

This level playing field makes a big difference to internal candidates who may initially be a bit suspicious that we will be more likely to promote candidates that we've uncovered. It's important for them to know, at the outset, that our interview process is as fair and unbiased as possible.

A CLIENT'S PERSPECTIVE

Throughout this book, I've introduced you to Eden Higgins, one of Duffy Group's practice leaders. What you may not know is that

Eden was once a client, and so she can bring to recruiting a deep knowledge base of what it's like to be on the other side of the recruiting process, needing talent to fill opportunities in her organization.

Eden's experience includes working with contingency recruiters who quickly produced long lists of candidates for her review. "There was no deep dive," she said, "because they hadn't invested the time to find out what I was really looking for. They were using a job description and a résumé and trying to match it up."

Eden is now a firm believer in the value of the recruitment research methodology, particularly when it comes to comparing external and internal candidates.

"The interview process is the same, the deep dive is the same," she said.

Our experience with filling a higher education position for a university in South Carolina is helpful to consider here. There were two internal candidates for the position, and we had uncovered several passive candidates. We provided the client with a grid that measured all the qualifications they had indicated were critical for the position. Frankly, the internal candidates were simply not as strong as the external candidates. But the client didn't have to take our word for it or trust us when we said that the candidates we had uncovered were better. They could see it for themselves in the data we provided.

Recruitment research didn't simply equip them to identify the best candidate for a single opportunity. As a result of our deep dive into their internal candidates, they now had additional information about their internal team members—information that they can use to identify other opportunities where they might be a better fit.

I'll talk more about how recruitment research enables you to build a talent pipeline later in the book. For now, let's spend a bit more time discussing the evaluation process and how we prepare clients to take the final candidates over the finish line.

PASSING THE BATON

I've talked a lot about the customization options offered by the recruitment research methodology. Each client may need different pieces of the puzzle, relying on us for the deep dive, an initial vetting, or sometimes just the strategic research we'll discuss more in the next chapter.

This means that we don't have a one-size-fits-all approach to the handoff to clients, but there are certain key elements that I can share with you. First of all, we ask the same interview questions of all candidates. These questions are based on the intake data our clients share with us at the start of the search—the critical qualifications and elements of cultural fit that are particularly important for this opportunity. If one or more of those questions has revealed some specific insight—some element that will be important for our client to recognize in assessing candidates—we need to make certain that those questions are asked of all candidates. We also ask the questions in the same order, again trying to avoid any circumstance where our process may create inequity in how candidates are evaluated.

Interview notes are a part of the package that clients are given at the handoff. These include the questions that were asked as well as a résumé and profile for each candidate.

Next, we get into some of the specifics that are unique to the position and to our client's requirements. Some opportunities might require that our package includes a project list, more details about the candidates' skills and experience that are particularly pertinent to the opportunity. We include a deal sheet if the opportunity involves financing or selling. There will be other addendums for specific fields. For some opportunities—an attorney search is one example that comes to mind—clients want the candidates to provide a writing sample. For a graphic artist, it might be a design sample. Strong letters of recommendation are often part of the interview notes. Sometimes even a well-written cover letter will help a client identify the best candidate, and so that's included.

For the South Carolina university opportunity I referenced earlier, we created a web portal with résumés, profiles, and our candidate spreadsheet. This is an incredibly valuable resource for hiring leaders; it means that members of the search committee can access the candidate information at any time to review the data they'll need to make the best hiring decision.

Some clients take a just-the-facts approach. For those clients, we create bulleted notes that summarize the key points from the interview. This is a real time-saver for clients who need to fill multiple positions and want to be able to quickly assess and compare candidates. They don't want to page through a lot of details; we understand this and can highlight the most important data. For other, higher-level positions, the client may need and want as much data as possible; for those clients, we include the deep-dive information that's been uncovered for each candidate.

Many recruiters present a list of all candidates at once. That's not our approach. We prefer to present candidates in real time, as we uncover and vet them. We interview them, and if the client requests it, we do our deep dive. Once we've confirmed that they're qualified, interested, and a good fit, we send them on to the client.

Of course, there are exceptions. Some opportunities—particularly at the CEO level—require a different submission process. It may be because boards meet on a specific schedule, and they want to

REVOLUTIONIZING RECRUITMENT

be able to review all candidates at once. In those cases, we will compile a complete roster of candidates and then present them all together.

I said at the start of this chapter that we're agnostic when it comes to this handoff stage. This also means that, when we present a list of candidates to our client, we don't rank them. We clearly state to our clients, when presenting the list, that the candidates are arranged in alphabetical order, or in order of interviews, or simply in no particular order. We know that our clients need to make that final decision and rank the candidates in order of their preference, not ours.

We know that our clients need to make that final decision and rank the candidates in order of their preference, not ours.

Our final slate is generally a roster of three to five candidates. There are exceptions of course, depending on the number of skilled candidates and the opportunity. We recently performed a CEO search in which our final slate listed eight qualified candidates. That slate included their names, titles, current employers, and—at the start—a note indicating that the candidates were being presented alphabetically, not in order of merit.

Eight candidates are more challenging to compare in detail. When we have more extensive slates like that one, we create a comparison chart that gives our client snapshot details of the most critical skills for the position. We had specific snapshots comparing the candidates based on budgetary responsibility. We noted which candidates had prior CEO experience and those for whom this would present an opportunity for advancement. We stated their highest earned academic degree, their salary, and a few other specifics that would be especially helpful to our client in quickly assessing this particular slate of candidates.

We know that it's not our assessment of the candidates that ultimately carries the most weight. It's the client's assessment.

Do clients ask for our opinion? Of course they do. And when they ask for it, we share our thoughts willingly but not when we present that slate. Those kinds of frank discussions take place after our client has had a chance to review the candidates first and to form their own opinion. Then we're happy to share our feedback if it's invited. And the good news is that, in nearly every case, we discover that we are all on the same page.

NEXT STEPS

It may have been an ongoing process over two to three weeks, or we may have provided all candidates at once. But regardless of how the candidates are presented, we want to support our clients in the final steps of the interview process as an offer is extended—and, we hope, accepted.

The hiring leaders provide us with vital information at the start of the recruiting process as they complete our intake forms and throughout our initial conversations about their requirements for the position. But the feedback they give us once the candidate slate has been presented is every bit as critical.

Our goal is to get feedback within twenty-four hours of a candidate first being presented—specifically, whether they like the candidate, and what prompted this response. But that isn't always possible, so we push to get that feedback, as quickly as possible, to help us determine whether additional criteria need to be added to the search, whether new candidates must be identified, and what our client's response is to the work that's been performed so far. It may be in the form of a meeting or a conference call—each recruiter has a slightly different approach for these follow-up conversations—but it's critical for us to have these touch points to measure the success of the search.

Every hiring leader is different. Every company has its own methods and hiring practices. Our goal is to have a conference call with every hiring leader involved in the search to assess our progress and to identify any additional steps that might be needed.

We want to know the answer to the question "What did you think of this person?" And also to this one: "Are we moving in the right direction?" Our goal is to move candidates quickly through the process, get them interviewed by hiring leaders, and then—we hope—get them hired.

Our work doesn't end when the slate of candidates is presented. Some clients ask us to schedule their interviews with candidates. Some clients want us to be present and participate in those interviews. Some ask us to check candidate references. Some want us to prepare interview guides, with key questions that may help them identify the best fit.

For certain high-level searches, especially those involving a board, we prepare not only the questions that will be asked but also specify which board member will ask which question. This ensures that the same board members ask each candidate the same question, to guarantee that uniformity of candidate presentation and vetting.

There's a lot of customization in recruitment research, so let me stop here and underscore one constant, no matter when the handoff to the client happens: our excitement and enthusiasm for the research we're providing.

We've spent time getting to know our clients and the specific needs of their organization. And we've invested time and effort in identifying the very best candidates for that opportunity.

By the time we present those candidates to our client, we're confident that they have the right qualifications to do the job—and they're interested in the opportunity. That's an exciting service—matching the right client and the right opportunity to the right candidate. And we communicate that enthusiasm.

It's not forced or fake. That's why the feedback is so important for us. We're eager to share what we've discovered with our client, and we're excited to learn their response.

Practice leader Sharon Grace uses the analogy of being a match-maker. "Sometimes I'll start talking about a candidate even before I get their résumé. My client knows that I've found someone great, and they're looking forward to seeing that résumé and learning more about them. It's like we're setting up that first date. Both parties are curious and interested and can't wait to meet."

Like a good matchmaker, we don't just throw two people together and step back to see what happens. We actively prep both parties to make sure that they have the tools and the data they need to make a great first impression.

I've discussed the data that we provide clients, but let me take a moment here to share some of the prep work that we do with candidates before their interviews. If we're handling scheduling interviews, then our prep call with candidates can happen as soon as the interview has been scheduled and confirmed. When our client is scheduling interviews, we arrange a prep call as soon as their interview has been booked.

These prep calls are generally brief, although with some senior-level searches, they might take more time and involve more preparation. But they provide an opportunity for us to go back and revisit our discussion about the organization and the role for which they are interviewing. We touch on the important parts of that role—in some cases, it may have been a few weeks since we last spoke, so it's helpful to refresh their memory. We may review what we uncovered during our last conversation or conversations with them. We highlight the elements of their background and strengths that are most pertinent to this opportunity. We share with them the questions that may come their way.

I've mentioned that feedback from clients is important, but we also debrief candidates. We want to hear from them after the interview—ideally, immediately after the interview, when they're sitting in their car and the details are still fresh. I want to know not only how they felt about the interview but also their response to the organization and the hiring leader.

The goal is to once more be an extension of our client's human resources team. Surprises can be great in life, but we do our best to minimize them in the interview process and up until that offer is extended and accepted.

The recruitment research methodology helps eliminate unexpected surprises as we hand off candidates to our client. The research equips us not only to vet candidates but also to understand their motivation, be deeply aware of the competitive landscape, and provide our clients with the data to ensure that a candidate is a good fit, highly qualified, and interested in this opportunity.

ACTION PLAN

- Consider your process for comparing external and internal candidates. Identify potential steps that may prevent candidates from being assessed in a thorough, apples-to-apples analysis.

- Before preparing interview questions, revisit the key skills and qualifications that are unique to this opportunity and devise questions that accurately measure these skills.

- Don't assume that applicants who interview for a job will accept an offer. Include an opportunity for candidate feedback at the end of an interview to measure interest and enthusiasm.

CHAPTER ELEVEN

WE WANT A LONG-TERM RELATIONSHIP

I've described the work we do as being a bit like matchmaking. We're not interested in making short-term connections for our clients. We want to identify candidates who will make a lasting contribution to their organization.

The same perspective is true for our own relationships with our clients. We're looking to marry, not date.

Our goal is to develop a partnership that lasts well beyond a client's immediate need to identify the best candidates for a vacancy. We are delighted to work with them to provide that service, but we want to do more. We are committed to building a relationship that supports them well into the future.

Practice leader Sharon Grace is the one who first coined that phrase at Duffy Group—"We're looking to marry, not date"—so I'll let her explain exactly how that thinking informs our practice.

"First, I think that it speaks to how thorough we are from the beginning," Sharon said. "We focus, during the intake process, on understanding what the hiring managers need. They want to hire someone not just for today's need but for the future. They need candidates to help meet those challenges and to support their efforts to scale their business. As we gather the information, as we discuss potential candidates with the hiring managers, we learn more about what it is that they're looking for and what interests them. That builds a connection and hopefully leads to a long-term relationship."

Whenever we talk to a client, we emphasize the fact that we want to be an extension of their team. That's what resonates for me when I think about our focus on building lasting connections with our clients. They trust us, they know that they can turn to us when they have a need, and they also know that we'll respect their input and their desire to participate. They know that we will work with them if they have an internal candidate, and we'll respect and vet that candidate with the same enthusiasm—and thoroughness—that we would bring to an external candidate who we had identified.

That trust piece also means that they can turn to us if they identify a great candidate who is currently working for one of their competitors. They may not feel comfortable directly approaching that person, but they know that they can rely on us to make that approach and to accurately assess any interest. The recruitment research approach supports this—our clients can hire us to perform any step in the recruitment research process they need, knowing that they will be billed only for the time we spend and only for the specific services they want.

A result of building these kinds of long-term relationships is that we really get to know our clients. We understand how their organizations work, and we learn the kinds of candidates who succeed in that culture. This means that we create an almost invisible link. When we talk to candidates, when we interview them or compile competitive research, there is a nearly seamless transition from us to the candidate to the client and back. We can represent our clients with a databank of extensive knowledge, compiled as a result of many conversations. Candidates don't have the sense that they're interacting with a third party; they often don't recognize that we are not physically a part of our client's organization.

That's our goal, that seamless transition. That's the result of a long-term relationship, or a marriage.

Practice leader Colleen Neese spent more than two decades working in retained executive search before learning about recruitment research and becoming an enthusiastic convert to the benefits of its efficiency and cost savings. She reflects on the value of creating long-term relationships between client and candidate as a side effect of the lasting relationships we've created with our clients.

"We want to do our best work for our clients," she explained. "We don't want to put people into their organizations who are only going to be there for a few months. I don't consider it a success until the hired candidate has been in the role for at least a year. I measure success by whether this person is going to be a successful member of the team well into the future."

The recruitment research approach means that we can shift our focus away from getting a quick placement to a more lasting form of human resources support. We pay attention to culture, avoiding the temptation to fit a square peg into a round hole. We think about our client's strategic needs as well as the evolving marketplace in which they are operating.

The recruitment research approach means that we can shift our focus away from getting a quick placement to a more lasting form of human resources support.

TOUCH POINTS

Just like a good marriage, we're helping our clients build a solid foundation, but we're also preparing for the future. As one search narrows to the final candidate list, we often talk to our clients about what's next. We talk to HR managers, to hiring leaders, reviewing our progress in the current search while identifying potential areas where we can offer other support—needs they may not have fully identified yet but opportunities where our expertise will add value. We review their website to analyze any positions they may be advertising that might be a good match for a candidate we presented who didn't meet their final criteria but who would be a great fit for another position within their organization.

As the search ends, as they begin to build a relationship with their newly hired candidate, we shift our focus to supporting and nurturing our relationship, making sure that they are pleased with our work and looking ahead to future opportunities to continue to partner with them.

We don't let too much time go by before reconnecting. We want to confirm that our research was successful, that they're pleased with the hire. Whenever possible, we transition from one project to another within an organization, ensuring that our partnership continues to grow and our ability to understand and represent our client stays fresh.

When that isn't possible—for a smaller organization, for example, whose staffing needs are more cyclical and infrequent—we touch base with both the client and the candidate about forty-five days after the start date. It's an opportunity to confirm that the hire was successful and that both parties are pleased. We'll follow up again after about sixty or ninety days, checking in and discussing any future needs.

We also like to share feedback from one party to the other. For instance, if a client praises a new hire's accomplishments, we share that with the hire. If the employee reports something exciting about their organization, we want our client to know that their employee is engaged and enthusiastic. The opportunities to give feedback are ongoing; we want that relationship to continue to develop while we ensure that our relationship with the client is also fostered.

We might remind them to take a look at the spreadsheet of candidates we provided as future vacancies arise. We want them to know that that resource is theirs, continuing to deliver value.

The relationship begins with an initial phone call and a first conversation. But it continues with phone calls and check-ins long after the hire has been finalized. We want our clients to be happy. We want their newly hired employees to be engaged. And we want our research to support future decision-making.

THE RESEARCH REPORT

I'd like to focus a little more intently on how we report our research to clients, as the terms can sometimes be confusing. Every recruitment research firm does things a bit differently, but at Duffy Group our model is to continuously deliver the results we uncover to our clients.

I mentioned earlier that we often present candidates in real time rather than waiting to assemble a single list of all qualified candidates. This steady flow of information and data is also true of our recruitment research. We communicate with clients in many different ways; one key way is our weekly update that details the progress of the search. It's essentially a status report that explains every step we've taken in support of their search during that week as well as what's on tap for the week ahead. This report lists precisely how many people we've talked to, who is interested and who isn't, and why. It details the hours we've spent on the search and what time we anticipate dedicating to it in the week ahead.

This is a unique model. Retained and contingency search firms don't provide these sorts of highly detailed and specific updates. It's a way to deliver our promise to our clients that our search will be economical and efficient and to allow them continuous opportunities to track their budget and confirm that it aligns with the expenses of the search.

Trust and integrity matter to me. I don't want clients to be surprised by unexpected costs. These weekly reports specify the number of hours we've dedicated to their search, and it's a rolling number so that they can easily see the work that's being performed on their behalf.

In the previous chapter, we talked about the candidate profiles we deliver at the interview stage, which provide specific information about the final slate of candidates our client will be considering and interviewing. Then, at the end of the search, we deliver a final research report, usually in the form of a spreadsheet that can be downloaded into their applicant tracking system. This is an incredibly valuable resource for our clients. It lists every person we spoke with and all the data that we gathered on them. It specifies their salary, their position, their current employer, and any reasons we uncovered that might inspire a particular passive candidate to consider a new opportunity.

With traditional recruiting firms, when they've been hired for a recruiting project and they've identified a group of candidates, they own that candidate database. With the recruitment research model, the reason our clients pay us by the hour is because we are creating a candidate database for them. That database becomes their property, a resource they can use that contains everyone with whom we spoke, their contact information, and any additional relevant data about them.

That final research report also contains market data—the kind of competitive data that helps the client to understand what their competitors are doing and the salaries and benefits they are offering employees. A client can learn about a competitor's incentives—do the salespeople get a company car or a car allowance? Which do they prefer? We uncover all sorts of incentives, from salary and bonus information to which companies are offering pawternity benefits, where employees are granted time off when they adopt a dog or cat to allow them to acclimate their new pet to its new home.

The value of this research report is clear: it can be used by our client's internal recruiting team moving forward without any additional billing on our part. The recruitment research is theirs, and it can be used to build a talent pipeline that meets future recruiting needs.

It's happened more than once that I'll notice that a client has posted an opportunity or mentions an anticipated role that they'll soon need to fill. I'll remind them of the research report we provided and suggest that they review the candidate database, especially when I know that at least one or two of the people we spoke with might be interested and qualified for this new opportunity. The client can review the information and, if they choose, do the outreach to those candidates themselves. Or, of course, they can hire us to do it for them.

We want to marry, not to date. We want to build a relationship with our clients that lasts well beyond a single opportunity and a single hire. Recruitment research is at the heart of that relationship.

ACTION PLAN

- Develop a candidate database with every recruitment campaign; archive qualified applicants who may be better suited to other opportunities or future needs.

- Check in with new hires at regular intervals, ideally thirty to forty-five days after they start. Ask specific questions and note areas where they are engaged and enthusiastic.

- Assess market data to ensure that your organization is offering competitive benefits, highlighting all differences. Periodically review existing benefits packages in comparison with this competitive data.

CHAPTER TWELVE

BUILDING YOUR TALENT PIPELINE

I've dedicated my career to connecting people. The recruitment research method has been a key component in this, enabling me to focus on providing strategic support to my clients and building long-term relationships with them. My goal is to equip them to identify the very best candidate for an opportunity, whether that results in an internal or external hire.

The recruitment research method also means that my clients receive valuable market data and a candidate database that allow them to hire for the future, equipping them to meet future staffing needs and identify those individuals who will support organizational growth and innovation.

I want my clients to have the tools and knowledge they need to build a talent pipeline. And I want the same for you.

As you've read through this book, I hope that you have begun to think strategically about your own human resources needs. My intent is for you to understand how recruitment research offers a new way of thinking about identifying the best candidate for an opportunity and to use the action plans at the end of each chapter to incorporate the key concepts into a strategy that makes sense for your recruiting process.

One of the best pieces of advice I can share is to make this a priority. View human resources as a vital part of your organization's strategic decision-making, and include preparations for future vacancies and opportunities in the visioning process. If at all possible, don't take a short-term view of recruitment, where it is attended to only when there is an immediate need. Let it be an ongoing process, where you are constantly preparing and planning for future opportunities with a vibrant and up-to-date candidate database.

I understand that it's not easy to devote that kind of time and effort to long-term planning when there are so many other demands and priorities. The work that we do takes time, and hiring leaders are busy. If your organizational size makes this feasible, dedicate a member of your human resources team to building a talent pipeline; it should be 100 percent of their job. It's that important. Their focus should be on developing relationships, researching competitors, and curating a talent database that is ready when there is a recruitment need.

Recognize that the specialists in your organization—those who are on-site day after day—have organizational and cultural knowledge that is unique. If you are one of those hiring leaders, I appreciate your unique perspective. You understand the pulse of the business; you know what your entire organization needs on a strategic level. You are participating in meetings; you hear what the

CEO and the executive team are discussing, or you are participating as a member of the executive team yourself. It may be a new product launch planned in three months. It may be a new market that has been identified, or a new facility that will open next year, or an acquisition that's being planned. The steady flow of your organization's growth and development has implications for hiring, and I encourage you to use that internal information as a springboard for your own recruitment activities. Start looking into what competitors are doing, start researching the market landscape, identifying salaries and incentives and even potential passive candidates. Leverage this internal knowledge into developing a talent pipeline well before the requisition is open and the opportunity needs to be posted. Prepare for your recruiting needs before you need to recruit. And if you need support, consider using a recruitment research expert like Duffy Group to help you build that pipeline.

Another tip is to think strategically about each connection you make and every candidate you consider. Don't simply view them through the lens of a single position. Assess their fit for your organization beyond one immediate opportunity. You may encounter a candidate for a managerial-level position who isn't quite strong enough to be hired as a manager but who has a great background and is an excellent cultural fit. Consider them for a supervisor role. Assess their interest in additional opportunities, and if it's there, determine how to leverage that interest.

Recruiting should not be a static, one-off process. No organization can afford to miss opportunities or to overlook great candidates. Wherever

> **Recruiting should not be a static, one-off process. No organization can afford to miss opportunities or to overlook great candidates.**

possible, maintain enough flexibility to rework positions and responsibilities so that you can always hire great people.

Recruitment research equips us to make those kinds of introductions, connecting great people with great organizations. Our view is that it's always better if those introductions happen sooner rather than later.

That's why our research report includes what we call *outliers*—candidates who may not be a perfect match for the qualifications that our client has stressed but who still could be an excellent addition to the organization. Sometimes we see trends in the market or a shifting landscape that informs our thoughts on a candidate and our sense of potential needs our client may identify in the future. We want their talent pipeline to be ready.

There's something fun and exciting about this kind of forecasting. We love to put the pieces of a puzzle together, to see who might fit and where. I encourage you to take this view, to think in fresh and creative ways about how people might be able to contribute to your organization and anticipate future needs.

That's why I feel that the recruitment research model is such a revolutionary tool. Our focus is on providing clients with information so that they can make not just one hire but multiple hires. Our research provides a framework for one search that they can use to build on for future searches.

LOOKING AHEAD

As I was completing the writing of this book, the coronavirus (COVID-19) suddenly and dramatically impacted the global economy. The virus continues to rage on, and there are lasting implications as COVID-19 forever changes the ways in which we live, work, and do business. Companies have been challenged to rethink their traditional business models, finding new approaches to operate differently and—in many cases—more efficiently. This requires a change in mindset for organizations accustomed to bringing their employees into the office every day who have had to pivot to a remote workplace. Many who did not fully embrace new technology are now doing business virtually using Zoom and other platforms, and non-profits and other businesses need to find creative ways (aside from major events) to raise funds for their organizations.

Many organizations have responded to the pandemic by reducing their workforce, and so, as a recruiter, I recognize that one likely outcome is an abundance of talent. The bigger talent pool presents an opportunity for hiring leaders, but sifting through hundreds of résumés to find the best fit will be even more laborious and time-consuming. A strategic approach is more important than ever, especially when the best candidate for your opportunity may be currently employed in another position.

As companies adapt to doing more with less, hiring the right people is critical. The wrong candidate can come at a hefty cost in training and employee morale, and organizations that are focusing on building a leaner, more efficient workforce will require skilled talent acquisition specialists to ensure that new hires are the best fit for every open position.

The economic picture is now clearer than it was when COVID-19 first struck, and hiring leaders can begin to take steps to prepare for what's next. It's true that the pandemic has impacted certain industries particularly hard—retailers, restaurants, and the hospitality industry, of course. But the good news is that the economic outlook for the US remains bright; the Congressional Budget Office has said that it expects gross domestic product to return to its prepandemic level by the middle of 2021.[9]

What does this mean for us as recruiters, and you as you build your talent pipeline? It means that the decision making about who to hire, and when, needs to be even more strategic and thoughtful. If fewer people are forming the core of your organization, if you're only going to add one person to a team or a board instead of three or four, you want a recruitment process that's steeped in research, so that you are positioned to identify the very best fit.

Before COVID-19, corporate leaders routinely told me that finding skilled workers was one of their biggest challenges. With more talented, highly skilled workers available, there's an opportunity for organizations to plan for their hiring needs before another talent drought. Companies that build a pipeline of talent and prepare for business in a post-pandemic environment will undoubtedly have a strategic advantage.

It's no surprise that candidates are looking for stability and safety when assessing a new opportunity, but with the uncertainty of COVID-19, these factors are even more vital. Organizations may find it helpful to focus on stability and safety within their culture, and stress these factors when reaching out to passive candidates.

One of our clients says it beautifully: "I believe that many of our new practices will be a permanent part of our value proposition to the communities we serve."

There will be increasing pressure on hiring leaders to adapt to meeting candidates and interviewing them remotely. We also anticipate a need for delayed starting dates for new hires. Loyal employees

---

9   Kate Davidson, "U.S. Economy Is Expected to Reach Pre-Pandemic Peak by Mid-2021," *Wall Street Journal*, February 1, 2021, https://www.wsj.com/articles/u-s-economy-expected-to-reach-pre-pandemic-peak-by-mid-2021-cbo-says-11612195200.

recognize that it may take more time for their replacement to be identified and hired, particularly during periods of remote working, and they may request and expect more time to transition from one organization to another.

Change can bring both opportunities and challenges. Organizations will need to be flexible and willing to adapt. And thoughtful, thorough research will be more important than ever to interpret shifting market landscapes—and identify great people.

HIRING FOR SUCCESS

I've spent a lot of time working with hiring leaders and executives who want to build strong teams, create more effective boards, and identify the best and the brightest for their organization. All of them want to know whether there is a specific formula, a framework to identify the right fit.

I shared some insight from Patrick Lencioni earlier and mentioned how much I admire him, so perhaps it's appropriate to share his strategy for hiring at the end of this book.

Lencioni argues that great organizations arise from great teamwork, and so his recommendation to hiring leaders and executives is to identify team players when searching for the best candidate for a new opportunity.[10] He states that team players have three vital characteristics: they are humble, hungry, and smart. He suggests focusing on these three areas when assessing whether to hire someone.

How can you do this? Lencioni's recommendation is to frame interview questions to draw out candidate responses in a way that

---

10   Patrick Lencioni, "Hiring Ideal Team Players," The Table Group, accessed July 2020, https://www.tablegroup.com/download/itp-hiring-guide.com.

will shed light on the presence or absence of these three areas. I'll share just a few of his key insights to get you started.

Humility can be measured by candidates who share credit and define success collectively; you will learn a lot by asking them to describe what they like and dislike about their current team.

When Lencioni lists *hungry* as a key attribute, he means candidates who are eager and ambitious, looking for the next opportunity. He suggests focusing on questions that will reveal candidates who are diligent and self-motivated. You may wish to inquire about their work ethic as a teenager, or ask them to specify the hours they typically work during a week.

Lencioni's third attribute is *smart*. This may seem an obvious marker for a great candidate, but it can be difficult to distinguish between candidates who are intelligent and candidates who have good judgment and are aware of the impact of their words and actions on other members of their team. You'll gain insight by asking them about how they handled a difficult boss or colleague.

Every hiring opportunity creates a chance to enhance your organization, so do your homework. Think carefully about your goals for this position. Identify the target, communicate that target to all who are partnering with you in the hiring process, and create opportunities throughout that process to review, to give feedback, and to reconsider your strategy if the right people aren't being identified.

If you haven't used recruitment research before, I encourage you to be curious and to learn more. Meet with a recruitment research professional. Learn how this model can support your recruitment strategies.

I love what I do. I'm passionate about recruitment research. I believe in the model because it works.

The core concepts of recruitment research extend beyond simply hiring people. Understanding your market landscape, building your knowledge base, and assessing the impact of future growth are all critical for strategic decision-making. My hope is that you'll engage with these ideas in ways that make sense for your business, whether as part of an executive training or coaching program, in support of a new focus on team building, or as a step in preparing for organizational growth.

Recruitment research began as a revolutionary way of thinking about identifying the best talent. I hope that it's now part of your strategy for managing your organization's most valuable asset: its people.

ACTION PLAN

- Insert more flexibility into your organization's HR recruitment practices to create opportunities for talented candidates.

- Identify three key elements of your organization's strategic plan that will impact recruitment needs in the next year.

- Consider assessing key teamwork attributes as part of your interview process.

ADDITIONAL RESOURCES

I hope that you've been inspired to do your own deep dive into recruitment research and learn more. In this book, I've cited management experts and quoted recruiting professionals, plus I've shared some of the research I've uncovered that's shaped my thinking about identifying the right people for the right opportunity.

Here are the resources I've used as well as the links to some sites I've found helpful in writing this book.

RECRUITMENT RESEARCH PROFESSIONALS

Duffy Group Inc. (https://duffygroup.com): Throughout this book, I've shared not only my own perspective but also the creative insights of many of the practice leaders at Duffy Group, a certified woman-owned business. I'm proud of the work we do, and I invite you to visit our website to learn more about our team, our areas of expertise, and recruitment research.

Novo Group Inc. (https://thenovogroup.com): In this book, you read insights from recruitment research expert Kelly Renz. Kelly is the president and CEO of Novo Group. Their mission is to "help organizations solve complex people challenges by finding the talent you can't, and transforming the people you have."

SGA Talent (http://sgatalent.com): Sheila Greco is a recruitment research expert who kindly shared her perspective in this book. She is the CEO of SGA Talent, a certified minority-owned recruitment research and recruiting firm.

Thorn Network Inc. (https://thornnetwork.com): Amanda Piriano has worked in recruitment research since 1991, and I'm grateful for her willingness to share her expertise in these pages. She is the president and managing director of Thorn Network, a firm that focuses on partnering with organizations across the country to assist in surfacing candidates who are not responding to traditional recruiting methods.

SOURCES QUOTED IN THIS BOOK

Jeff Kavanaugh and Ravi Kumar, "How to Develop a Talent Pipeline for Your Digital Transformation," *Harvard Business Review*, November 27, 2019, https://hbr.org/2019/11/how-to-develop-a-talent-pipeline-for-your-digital-transformation.

Alison Konrad, *Organizational Culture, Values, and Fit in the Workplace: Making the Right Job Choices* (Ontario, Canada: Ivey Publishing, 2011).

John Ladley and Thomas C. Redman, "Use Data to Accelerate Your Business Strategy," *Harvard Business Review*, March 3, 2020, https://hbr.org/2020/03/use-data-to-accelerate-your-business-strategy.

Patrick Lencioni, "Hiring Ideal Team Players," The Table Group, accessed July 2020, https://www.tablegroup.com/download/itp-hiring-guide.

Patrick Lencioni, "What Clients Really Want," The Table Group, accessed July 2020, https://www.tablegroup.com/hub/post/what-clients-really-want.

LinkedIn Talent Solutions, "The Ultimate List of Hiring Statistics," accessed September 2020, https://business.linkedin.com/content/dam/business/talent-solutions/global/en_us/c/pdfs/Ultimate-List-of-Hiring-Stats-v02.04.pdf.

Michael Schneider, "7 LinkedIn Statistics That Will Make You Question Your Recruitment Strategy," *Inc.*, June 14, 2018, https://www.inc.com/michael-schneider/7-linkedin-hiring-trends-that-will-change-way-you-recruit.html.

John Sullivan, "7 Rules for Job Interview Questions That Result in Great Hires," *Harvard Business Review*, February 10, 2016, https://hbr.org/2016/02/7-rules-for-job-interview-questions-that-result-in-great-hires.

Teri Wilford Wood and Anna Broccolo, "New York Enacts Legislation Related to Board Diversity," *The National Law Review*, January 17, 2020, https://www.natlawreview.com/article/new-york-enacts-legislation-related-to-board-diversity.